Liners in Battledress

Europa, wearing the dazzle colouring which had been applied for her participation in Operation Sealion.
(*United States National Archives*)

LINERS
IN BATTLEDRESS

Wartime Camouflage and Colour Schemes
for Passenger Ships

David Williams

CONWAY
MARITIME PRESS

Painting is the most astounding sorceress. She can persuede us through the most evident falsehoods that she is pure truth.

Jean Etienne Liotard

First published in Great Britain in 1989 by
Conway Maritime Press Ltd
24 Bride Lane, Fleet Street
London EC4Y 8DR

British Library Cataloguing in Publication Data

Williams, David
Liners in battledress: wartime camouflage
and colour schemes for passenger ships
1. Passenger ships, 1900–1983.
Camouflage & markings
I. Title
359.4

ISBN 0 85177 517 9

Designed by K & M Design Associates
Typeset by Swanston Graphics Ltd, Derby
Printed and bound in Great Britain by The Bath Press

Contents

Acknowledgements

The successful completion of any book depends to a great extent on the help given by others, often correspondents on the other side of the world who are rarely known personally by the author. This book is no exception; I have been the beneficiary of much valuable assistance and enthusiastic support in writing about this very complex and technical subject, and I can assure the reader that any inaccuracies are entirely my own.

It would be impossible to list here everyone I have spoken or written to in the course of preparing the book. However, there are a number of persons and organisations whom I should like to mention for their especially generous help.

For supplying me with vital photographs and information, a special thank you to five long-term friends and correspondents: Frank Braynard, Richard de Kerbrech, Arnold Kludas, L L von Münching and Tom Rayner.

A number of organisations very kindly placed their records at my disposal. They are Compagnie Générale Maritime, Comité International de la Croix-Rouge, Eastman Kodak, General Electric Company, Ministry of Defence Naval Historical Library, Royal Academy of Arts, Royal Naval Museum, Portsmouth and the Admiralty Research Establishment, Teddington, Middlesex.

For their assistance in locating and supplying photographs above and beyond the call of duty, my thanks to Paul Kemp at the Department of Photographs, Imperial War Museum, and Cliff Persons of the World Ship Photo Library. For producing the camouflage design elevations in Appendices 1 and 3, my thanks to Angie and Robin Groves.

My thanks to Robert Sumrall and the United States Naval Institute Proceedings for their kind permission to refer to and quote from Mr Sumrall's excellent articles on wartime camouflage, and to Captain Joseph McCleary of the United States Embassy, Captain A E Becker of the United States Naval Sea Systems Command and Dana Wegner of the David W Taylor Naval Ship Research & Development Center, Bethesda, Maryland.

Finally, owing to the evident interest in my project shown by George Prichard, Assistant Director at GEC Research Limited, I was put in touch with two of that company's former physicists, Jack Waldram and W Stevens OBE, who had worked with the late Alphonse Emile Schuil at Wembley before and during World War II. From them I learnt of the Schuil Memorial Photometer, an instrument designed by Mr Schuil and completed by his team after his death, as a tribute to this affectionately remembered man, each individual fabricating a piece by his or her own hands. It remains on display at the Hirst Laboratories.

In keeping with the sentiment symbolised by the Schuil Memorial Photometer, I hope that my book may be regarded as a small but fitting tribute to all those scientists, artists and engineers who devoted their energies to developing effective camouflage for use at sea.

Introduction

FROM VIRTUALLY the beginning of the age of steam at sea, merchant passenger vessels have been appropriated during times of war to perform auxiliary duties in support of armed forces. In this work they have served their countries' needs throughout these periods of adversity as dutifully and successfully as they served those of international trade and travel in more halcyon times.

Indeed, ocean passenger ships have proved to be so suitable for emergency work, with their vast and readily adaptable accommodation spaces and high speeds, often superior to contemporary warships, that in wartime they have been converted to serve in many very different capacities – as troopships, auxiliary cruisers, hospital ships, commerce raiders, accommodation ships and aircraft carriers, as well as in a number of even more specialised roles.

But for all their suitability, passenger liners were never intended to endure the rigours of sea warfare. As far as is known, none have ever been constructed with armour plating, anti-torpedo bulges or any other structural features which might have afforded them a measure of protection from attack. Even those vessels built with government subsidies and designed with auxiliary employment in mind lacked all but some hull stiffening and deck reinforcement for a number of gun emplacements and, perhaps, a slightly superior standard of hull subdivision.

Possibly the only inherent attribute of the merchant passenger liner which has contributed to its well-being during wartime was the high speed which peacetime competition on the world's passenger routes had invariably demanded of it. Whereas the award of a Blue Riband trophy may have represented a nebulous form of prestige in commercial terms, the knots which gained that acclaim assumed a far greater significance when they provided the means to outstrip an enemy submarine.

In recognition of the vulnerability to attack of the majority of passenger ships and other merchantmen called up for war service, some means of concealment was regarded as essential for their protection. Increasingly, they had their commercial livery obscured in order to render them, like warships, less conspicuous on the high seas, a measure that was relatively simple to implement.

Initially, this was achieved by the application of an overall coat of grey paint of some shade or other, a colour that was both cheap and plentiful, and easy to apply. On the face of it such a measure of camouflage appeared to be effective enough in practice. Certainly it was as effective as any static method of protection was expected to be and it was

Before 1917, auxiliaries of all types were painted in shades of plain grey. Here the *Justicia*, the former *Statendam*, displays her drab war livery. Later, she was repainted in dazzle colours. (*Imperial War Museum*)

The troopship *Huntsgreen*, the former Norddeutscher Lloyd *Derfflinger* seized by the British Government in October 1914. She too only wears a coat of neutral grey. (*CPL*)

generally considered adequate. However, following the outbreak of World War I, the first conflict in which ships were subjected to attack by submarine on a large scale, the progress of the war at sea soon indicated otherwise.

By mid-1917, allied shipping losses were at a critical level as a result of Germany's policy of unrestricted submarine warfare, threatening the collapse of the entire war effort. This grave situation was a result of much more than ineffective camouflage and, to bear this out, the introduction of convoy practices had an immediate impact on the situation. But without question it had also demonstrated that a coat of plain grey paint was invariably an inadequate form of concealment for unarmed merchantmen, whether sailing alone or in convoy.

The achievement of effective camouflage at sea was not easy, being fraught with unique problems. The constantly changing appearance of the environment in different circumstances of light, atmosphere and weather rendered the development of an all-purpose concealment measure an impossibility.

However, necessity being the mother of invention, there was no shortage of suggestions as to how the shipping losses could be reduced by improving maritime camouflage techniques. The Admiralty therefore established, through the Directorate of Naval Equipment, a special section to investigate and implement these ideas. Soon after, following the British lead the United States Navy Department's Bureau of Construction and Repair also set up a Camouflage Research Center. Its brief was to conduct research into alternative, more effective colour schemes, the objectives being either to reduce target visibility or to confuse target identity and heading. The result of all these actions was a range of innovative and often striking camouflage schemes, launching what in effect was a new art form and a completely new school of scientific research.

One group of schemes advocated soft hues and subtle textures, with the emphasis on precise colour blending, to create an optical illusion simulating invisibility. Others

The *Mauretania* in her distinctive 'patch-work' dazzle scheme. Disruptive and confusion paint schemes were in vogue in the later stages of World War I and for long periods of World War II. (*Imperial War Museum*)

proposed Dazzle painting, as it became popularly known, which called instead for ships to be painted in bright, contrasting colours, in strong geometric shapes, to make it difficult for a submariner to determine their bearing, speed or identity.

The teams of camouflage advisers assembled on both sides of the Atlantic comprised both artists and scientists and their approaches to the problem reflected the diversity of their backgrounds. One school of painters examined camouflage in the natural world and sought to apply the principles of protection in animal and plant colouring to these mechanical objects. More fundamentally, the scientific fraternity sought a deeper understanding of the very concept of visibility as a basis for devising methods by which it could be manipulated or distorted. Their studies led to the formulation of the first methods of quantitative measurement of visibility and of comparative assessment of the effectiveness of camouflage measures.

From these early experiments numerous, highly sophisticated and carefully devised disruption patterns were subsequently developed, providing the basis for the camouflage tactics that were adopted during World War II. Painted disguise or concealment was known as static camouflage. Dynamic camouflage, or the alteration of a ship's appearance by the addition, modification or removal of masts, funnels and other physical features, was also employed as an extension to painted deception in a further bid to outwit enemy submarines and surface raiders.

World War I also saw the introduction to certain large passenger ships of paint schemes that were intended to achieve the opposite effect of concealment or confusion. As approved schemes under the Geneva and Hague Conventions they were designed both to enhance the visibility and aid the identification of special categories of vessel. On the one hand, there were the neutrality markings of ships of non-belligerent nations attempting to go about their lawful, commercial business; on the other, there were the colour schemes applied to passenger vessels engaged on duties under the auspices of the International Red Cross, such as hospital ships and, later, diplomat repatriation ships.

All these schemes, along with other approaches to disguise and deception are

The American hospital ship *Red Cross* (ex-*Hamburg*) at Falmouth in September 1914. Unusually, for a World War I hospital ship, she has Red Crosses on her funnels but not on her sides. She later served as the hospital ship *Powhatan*. (*Tom Rayner*)

In contrast, Royal Mail Line's *Asturias*, British hospital ship number 2, does not display a Red Cross on her funnel which is also painted buff, not white. (*Tom Rayner*)

described in the following sections. Historical information on the research and development side of marine camouflage and colouring are incorporated in the main text preambles and, in the Appendices, details are provided of the official measures adopted by the Allies in both World Wars. These official schemes were applied to all types of vessel, both combatant and non-combatant, although in many instances they were never used on passenger ships. Nevertheless, this information has been included both for its general interest and because of its direct relevance to the subject.

Such an anomaly does, however, beg some explanation as to why this book concentrates almost exclusively on passenger vessels when many other ship types were also given camouflage treatment. Besides my own intense interest in passenger liners, there are a number of other very good reasons for focusing on this type of vessel.

First, for purposes of comparison, no other group of ships was painted in so many different wartime colour schemes, some individual vessels having received as many as three, four or five changes of livery. For instance, Cunard's record-breaker *Mauretania* was painted in three different colour schemes during World War I. Her fleetmate *Aquitania*, which saw active service in both World Wars, had her appearance altered no fewer than five times in the course of her auxiliary career, while the British troopship *Olympic* and the American troopship USS *Louisville* (ex-*St Louis*) were certainly not unique in having more than one camouflage scheme tried out on them experimentally during 1917 and 1918.

Secondly, from an official point of view, the painting of converted passenger ships in protective colouring was deemed to be especially vital. Of all merchantmen, the Admiralty gave the highest priority for camouflage painting to Armed Merchant Cruisers (AMCs) and troopships. Following America's entry into World War I, the Bureau of War Risk of the Treasury Department also considered it essential for all US-registered merchant vessels entering the war or submarine danger zones to be camouflaged but, due to the enormous number of vessels involved, an order of priority had to be established. This gave precedence to troop transports over all other types of ship. The Bureau also offered substantial discounts on insurance premiums for camouflaged passenger vessels operating in the war zone.

Finally, for the complexities and details of many of these colour schemes to be fully appreciated, they are best seen on the generally larger, uncluttered areas of the hulls and superstructures of passenger ships.

With the relentless march of progress, the need to perform troop carrying and other auxiliary operations by sea gradually diminished and the importance of effective visual camouflage simultaneously waned. After the end of World War II the regular transportation of troops to overseas garrisons was resumed by the United Kingdom with its fleet of Ministry of Transport troop carriers, managed on their behalf by the P&O, Bibby and British India Lines, and by the United States with its vast numbers of war-built P2 transports of the Military Sea Transportation Service. Increasingly, however, these vessels were dispensed with as aircraft took over the role of troop ferrying. It was not until the Falklands conflict that a requirement once more arose for merchant vessels to undertake auxiliary operations in support of active service units. In this respect, the clock had been indubitably turned back but in the lack of necessity for camouflage protection, the situation had actually turned full circle.

Among the passenger ships requisitioned for the South Atlantic Task Force were the *Queen Elizabeth 2*, *Canberra*, *Rangatira* and *Uganda*. The *Uganda*, which was designated the role of hospital ship, *was* painted in the appropriate livery, (white hull with green band and prominent red crosses) but the others, which served as troop carriers, remained in their company colours throughout. On the face of it, given the haste with which the ships had been prepared for sea, this was an understandable oversight, but there was, in fact, sound reasoning behind this apparent omission. With modern missile weapons able to strike a target beyond the horizon, without it first having to be sighted, the provision of painted camouflage protection was clearly a waste of both time and money. In a sense, this takes us back to the very earliest engine-propelled merchant

Starboard side view of White Star's *Olympic* in her first dazzle colour scheme. (*Imperial War Museum*)

auxiliaries, which were also left in their commercial livery for the duration of their engagement on military duties.

The reasoning behind this earlier deficiency was quite similar; it too was determined by the performance of contemporary ordnance. The muzzle loading naval guns of the early Victorian era had such a limited range that camouflage had no practical value to a vessel once it was within hitting distance of an enemy warship. Equally, for as long as the ship remained safely beyond that range, it was just as unnecessary.

The Great White Whale, P&O's *Canberra*, surrounded by well-wishing small craft at Southampton, on her return from the Falklands. Apart from a helicopter flight deck, she was structurally unaltered. (*Tom Rayner*)

AS FAR as possible, I have tried to keep detailed technical matter in the book to a minimum but, in order to provide a clear interpretation of a particular point, in a few instances this has proved unavoidable. This is the case, for example, in Part 2, in the explanations of colour synthesis and the vision process. The description of the Naval Camouflage Viewing Range in Part 3 is another example. A Glossary of Terms has been provided to assist the reader in understanding the technical expressions used. This incorporates the original Glossary of Camouflage Terms compiled by the General Electric Company for the Admiralty during World War II.

This, then, is a picture history of passenger ships at war, their numerous guises and disguises – a record of yeoman service, scientific ingenuity and artistic innnovation. It is also the story of the background to ship colouring conventions and of the research effort that has taken place to develop and understand camouflage techniques.

David L Williams
Newport, Isle of Wight
1989

The Victorian Age

THE PASSENGER STEAMSHIP had barely come of age when it was first called upon to perform auxiliary duties. Only thirty-five years after the *Savannah* had made the inaugural steam-assisted crossing of the Atlantic, the Crimean War (1854-1856) called for the first large-scale transportation of troops overseas by steam-driven vessels. Among the very earliest passenger steamships taken over to ferry troops throughout this campaign were P&O Line's famous *Himalaya*, one of the largest vessels of her day, and Brunel's iron screw steamer *Great Britain*.

The *Himalaya* proved to be so useful in this role that the Navy eventually purchased her outright. Indeed, she enjoyed an extremely long career with the Senior Service, latterly as a coal hulk, until she was bombed and destroyed by the Luftwaffe at Portland in June 1940.

As for the *Great Britain*, she had her accommodation modified to permit her to carry up to 1,650 soldiers and thirty horses on each voyage to Sevastopol. The large Crimean trooping fleet also included twelve Cunard ships and numerous other vessels from the P&O, Royal Mail and other fleets, all requisitioned by the Admiralty under the terms of the mail subsidy contracts concluded with these companies.

At the same time the distinction of being the first commercial passenger vessels to serve as hospital ships went to the Cunard Line ships *Andes* and *Cambria*. While Florence Nightingale was introducing improved standards of hygiene to the hospital wards ashore in the Crimea, these ships were employed to evacuate casualties away from the war zone from Balaclava to Scutari, Malta and Gibraltar, thus becoming the first of their kind to undertake this valuable work. Theirs were only very basic conversions, however; they were not hospital ships in the modern sense. Conditions on board were often insanitary, with widespread cholera among casualties and crew necessitating regular fumigation with sulphur. Britain's first true hospital ships were the Union Line's

The former P&O steamer *Himalaya* as a naval trooper. She is seen here with a white hull. (*CPL*)

The P&O steamer *Bengal*, requisitioned as a Crimean War troopship and seen here, during her military service, at Malta in 1853. (*CPL*)

The first iron screw steamer, Brunel's *Great Britain*, which served as a troopship during the Crimean War from 7 March 1855 to 7 January 1856. (*SS Great Britain Project*)

Spartan and *Trojan*, P&O's *Egypt*, the *Orcana* of the Pacific Steam Navigation Company and the *Maine*, first of five ships of this name to serve as British hospital ships, all of which were chartered for the duration of the Second Boer War (1899-1902). Two years earlier, the first American hospital ships, the *Missouri*, *Bay State*, *Relief* and *Solace*, all converted liners, were fitted out for the duration of the Spanish American War (1897).

For the record, the first auxiliary cruiser conversion did not occur until the 1860s. This was the *Vanderbilt*, popularly known as 'Commodore Cornelius Vanderbilt's flagship', and the fifth and largest vessel of the Vanderbilt European Line. On the outbreak of the American Civil War (1861-1865) she was taken over to serve as an auxiliary cruiser, becoming the first passenger steamship to be converted for a strictly naval role.

Whereas the nineteenth century witnessed the earliest cases of merchant passenger vessels being taken over for auxiliary purposes, this was less important, in the context of

The screw steamer *Andes* which, with her Cunard fleetmate *Cambria*, were the first steam passenger ships to be converted for hospital ship duties. (*University of Liverpool, Cunard archives*)

The *Cambria*. Unlike the steel-hulled *Andes* she was a paddler. (*University of Liverpool, Cunard archives*)

The first hospital ship to bear the name *Maine*, formerly of the Atlantic Transport Line. (*Imperial War Museum*)

The Collins Line record-breaking paddle steamer *Baltic* was among the mercantile passenger ships drafted into trooping service in the American Civil War, being conveniently available following her owner's financial collapse. (*CPL*)

The *Vanderbilt*, the first passenger steamship to be operated as an auxiliary cruiser. (*CPL*)

camouflage and protective colouring at sea, than other parallel developments which had a profound influence on these matters in the following century. The external appearance of these early troopships and auxiliary cruisers was probably not altered anyway. Certainly, no policy had been determined at that time regarding the deliberate and intentional use of disguise or concealment practices. This was primarily because there was then little practical value in having protective colouring of any description. Once a ship came within the relatively limited range of contemporary warships' guns she would have been both easily identifiable and sinkable whether she was camouflaged or not. By the same reasoning, if she remained beyond that range she had no real need for camouflage. As for hospital ships, it was still a long time before vessels of this type enjoyed an internationally respected immunity from attack, which necessitated the wearing of a distinct and recognisable livery.

Camouflage is an ancient practice, in a military sense, concerned with concealing what there is and suggesting what there is not. As far as can be determined, it was not until almost the turn of the century that any passenger ship taken over for auxiliary employment was afforded a measure of protective colouring. The first ships to benefit, by the application of a coat of plain grey paint, were the auxiliary cruisers *Harvard* (ex-*New York*), *Yale* (ex-*Paris*), *St Louis* and *St Paul*, formerly of the American Line, all of which were commandeered by the United States Navy to patrol and protect the supply lines to the armies fighting the Spanish on the islands of Cuba and the Philippine Archipelago during the Spanish American War. During the Second Boer War, as Britain was not facing a challenge at sea from a naval power, no such effort was made to disguise or conceal British passenger ships pressed into service for the duration. The only distinguishing feature of the ships taken over for the South African campaign, which were used principally for troop carrying, was their auxiliary number, painted on their sides in black

The *Spartan* ... (*World Ship Photo Library*)

... and the *Trojan* were among the first true hospital ships, taken up for the Second Boer War. The *Trojan* is shown in hospital ship livery – see the Red Cross symbol by the number on her bow quarter. (*World Ship Photo Library*)

characters on a white rectangular patch.

Even British steam warships of the Victorian era were not camouflaged or painted in any way to render them less visible. Their colour schemes, as revealed by paintings of contemporary Naval Reviews at Spithead, comprised black hull, white upperworks and buff or black funnels, colours that even had a rather commercial or merçantile look about them.

The introduction of comprehensive camouflage and protective colouring practices

The *Yale* (ex-*Paris*) auxiliary cruiser during the Spanish American War, sailing from Hampton Roads to Santiago on 23 June 1898. (*Frank Braynard*)

were, however, imminent. The seeds had been sown over the preceding 50 years through a series of peace conferences and major developments in naval weapons. The formulation of specific policies regarding the application of passenger ships to military support roles also played their part. The process began with the Declaration of Paris in April 1856, the treaty which formally terminated the Crimean War. This laid down the first conditions relating to the confinement and transportation of war invalids. It was an important milestone in the establishment of more humane treatment of prisoners and casualties generally and it became the foundation stone for the later, wider-sweeping provisions of the Geneva and Hague Conventions.

The Declaration of Paris also brought to an end, by international agreement, the practice of privateering, otherwise known as the *guerre de course*. This was the granting of a letter of marque or licence that permitted armed, privately owned vessels to operate against the merchant ships of an enemy and to seize as prize either the ships themselves or their cargo. A notable exception to the signatories of the Declaration was the United States of America. As a result, privateering continued to flourish during the American Civil War, causing grievous losses to both ships and lives. This was despite the fact that both the Unionists and Confederates actually showed a preference for taking over and arming merchantmen as regular warships.

During August 1864, some nine months before the end of the American Civil War, the European powers concluded an agreement at a peace conference at Geneva which established far-reaching legal provisions regarding the future treatment of sick and wounded servicemen and the status of those ministering aid to them. The Geneva Convention, as it was called, granted the first legal immunity from attack to all persons in these categories and to this end called for the prominent display of the Geneva Cross – a red cross on a white field, the reverse of the Swiss national flag – at all military hospitals, on ambulances and hospital trains and on the uniforms of all nurses and stretcher bearers.

The provisions of the Geneva Convention applied mainly to land warfare but a second conference at Geneva in October 1868 extended the principles of the agreement to embrace maritime conflict and the conveyance of casualties by sea. This was a development of great significance as far as those passenger ships destined to be employed in this capacity were concerned, although it was still some forty years before the wearing of distinctive colours by hospital ships was fully regulated. The Geneva Convention, prompted by Jean Henri Dunant, a Swiss citizen, also initiated the formation of the International Red Cross Society in 1870.

MEANWHILE, IN BRITAIN, in 1866, the Admiralty had formed its own Transport Department in a bid to retain a major element of its troop carrying commitment to the Army independent of commercial vessels. This followed recommendations based on the inadequacies of troop supply that had been experienced in the Crimean War and during the Sepoy Mutiny (1857-1858). A class of purpose-built naval transports resulted. Measuring 360ft in overall length, with a beam of 49ft and a draught of 20ft, their dimensions anticipated the opening of the Suez Canal. The five ships, named *Crocodile*, *Euphrates*, *Jumna*, *Malabar* and *Serapis*, each displacing 6,200 tons, represented a major improvement in troop accommodation and facilities. They were also the first vessels to display the colours that later became familiar on all peacetime troopships: white hull with coloured stripe and buff funnel. However, the coloured stripes on their hulls were not all the same, each vessel having its own colour, being respectively yellow, blue, red, black and green. It was not until later that the blue stripe was settled on as standard colouring for all vessels of the peacetime trooping fleet.

While the introduction of the *Crocodile* class of troopships proved satisfactory for the regular relief of the Indian Armies, any sizeable emergency undertaking continued to dictate an increasing dependence on the merchant service. Experience in the Zulu Wars (1879) and the First Boer War (1880-1881) clearly demonstrated this, suggesting that further changes to the nation's trooping arrangements were on the cards.

In this context the year 1894 was crucial for it saw the formal termination by the Admiralty of troop transportation on behalf of the Army by its own means. The Navy-owned trooping fleet was by then ageing and in a bad state of repair. No money was available to overhaul the ships or build replacements so the Admiralty's trooping service was disbanded completely and the decision made that all future wartime trooping duties would be performed by recruited mercantile passenger vessels. The owning companies were to be responsible for the manning, victualling and management of the ships, establishing an arrangement that has continued to the present day. Thereafter these ships were truly worthy of the description 'merchantmen at war'.

Her Majesty's Transport *Cephalonia*, Boer War troopship. (*World Ship Photo Library*)

Boer War troopships were repainted, where necessary, with black hulls. Shown here three more vessels taken over for the South African campaign. P&O Line's *Soudan*, number 13. (*CPL*)

... P&O Line's *Manila*, number 30, and ... (*CPL*)

In addition, certain selected shipping companies would be required to build specially designed trooper/liners for charter to the Admiralty in peacetime. The P&O and British India Lines were the first to take up this offer which guaranteed revenue in the slack period for scheduled services which to some extent coincided with the trooping season. Increasingly, however, the ships were laid up when not engaged on trooping to avoid the necessity of constantly modifying the accommodation spaces. Initially, the P&O vessels *Britannia* and *Rome*, and British India's *Dilwara* were taken up on charter but the first specially built, convertible ships, the *Assaye*, *Plassy* and *Sobraon*, entered service soon after, followed by the *Neuralia* and *Nevasa* in 1912 and 1913.

White Star Line's *Nomadic*, number 34. (*CPL*)

The *Britannia* hired transport number 3... (*CPL*)

... and the *Rome*, were the first P&O vessels to be chartered to the Admiralty for peacetime trooping. (*CPL*)

P&O's first three purpose-built peacetime troopships, the *Assaye*, troopship number 5 ... (*CPL*)

Sobraon ...
(*Real Photos*)

... and *Plassy*,
troopship
number 7.
(*CPL*)

**Between 1899 and 1902, during the Second Boer War, the *Assaye* was repainted black in contrast to her white colouring while engaged in the Indian trooping service.
(*CPL*)**

TWENTY-EIGHT YEARS earlier, in March 1885, the British attitude to the use of Armed Merchant Cruisers (AMCs) in wartime had been clarified by the 'Russian war scare'. When Russian troops invaded Afghanistan the British Government indicated its intention of intervening on the side of the Afghans, threatening the outbreak of full-scale war. In readiness, and in apparent conflict with the provisions of the Declaration of Paris concerning privateering, of which Britain was a signatory, sixteen passenger liners were prepared for employment as auxiliary cruisers because insufficient regular warships could be spared for the emergency:

**The second of British India's specially designed troopships, the *Nevasa* of 1913.
(*World Ship Photo Library*)**

Union Line's *Moor*, one of the two vessels commissioned as an auxiliary cruiser during the Russian War Scare. The other was ... **(*World Ship Photo Library*)**

Alaska	Guion Line	*Massilia*	P&O Line
America	National Line	*Mexican*	Union Line
Arizona	Guion Line	*Moor*	Union Line
Britannia	Pacific SN Co	*Oregon*	Cunard Line
Coptic	White Star Line	*Pembroke Castle*	Castle Line
Glenogle	Glen Line	*Rosetta*	P&O Line
India	British India SN Co	*Stirling Castle* (later *Nord America*)	La Veloce Line
Lusitania	Orient Line	*Umbria*	Cunard Line

Unlike the privateers that had existed prior to the Declaration of Paris, these merchant cruisers were to be commissioned as naval vessels throughout the period of their engagement and manned by service personnel. It was this distinction from the earlier privately owned and crewed vessels that permitted Britain to implement these conversions. The anomaly – for anomaly it was – surfaced in the later Hague Peace Conference when the use of vessels of this type was finally regulated.

The determination of Britain's response to the crisis had sufficient impact on the Russians to compel them to withdraw their forces from Afghanistan before the conflict escalated. In the event, only thirteen of the sixteen ships that had been appropriated

... Cunard Line's *Oregon*, previously a Guion Line Ship. (*CPL*)

completed their conversions. Of these, only two, Union Line's *Moor* and Cunard Line's *Oregon*, were actually commissioned.

Prior to the 'Russian war scare', the Admiralty had seen no particular merit in converting suitable commercial passenger vessels for use as auxiliary cruisers in times of national emergency. Having been compelled to pay a high price to hire ships on this occasion, many shipping companies were thereafter paid annual subsidies in return for agreeing to make their ships available whenever needed. An AMC register was compiled which listed all such vessels and by 1888 there were already twenty-seven liners earmarked for emergency service, among them the express units of the Cunard and White Star fleets as well as the latest ships to join the P&O, Anchor and Inman Lines.

Of the many developments that took place in the nineteenth century which influenced the adoption of camouflage techniques, the most important were those involving naval weaponry. The advances in gunnery throughout the Victorian era were dramatic. Breech loaders replaced muzzle loaders; broadside guns gave way to central batteries, which in turn gave way to revolving turrets on the centre line. Spherical shot became obsolete and conical projectiles fired from rifled artillery were introduced in its place. By the turn of the century the range of the heaviest main armaments had increased to almost 20 miles and, with accurate target spotting and direction finding, it was possible to hit and sink ships on the horizon. At these sorts of distances ships were in danger from the moment they became visible and it was no longer possible to consider range alone as providing protection.

More sinister was the development of the submarine and, to some extent in parallel, the self-propelled torpedo, without doubt the most potent conventional weapon combination ever contrived. Inventors had been working seriously on submersibles from the end of the eighteenth century, prominent among them being the American engineer Robert Fulton. The early designs were strictly limited in their capability, being unable to dive or operate totally under water. By the early 1900s, however, the first true submarines had been designed and built by John Philip Holland and these were already showing a close resemblance to the U-boats operated by Germany during World War I.

The self-propelled or locomotive torpedo was the brainchild of Robert Whitehead, an English marine engineer. With contra-rotating propellers driven by a clockwork motor (compressed air drive came later) and with a percussion operated explosive in its nose, it first went into production at the Royal Arsenal, Woolwich, in the mid-1870s.

Powerful guns had rendered merchant ships vulnerable to surface bombardment at extreme range. In the hidden menace of the torpedo-equipped submarine, the danger had been exacerbated, for the adversary could no longer be seen to be avoided. Some sort of

One of the vessels earmarked for service as an auxiliary cruiser during the 'Russian war scare' but which was not commissioned was Union Castle's *Mexican*. (*CPL*)

The *Nord America*, (ex-*Stirling Castle*), displaying in an unusual fashion, at her bows, her identity in this precise form. (*CPL*)

camouflage protection was now paramount and the matter became the subject of serious concern from around the late 1890s onwards. The white-hulled fleet of the United States 'Continental' Navy was repainted overall in a standard light grey. Simultaneously the vessels of the Grand Fleet had their hulls and superstructure overpainted with a darker shade of the same colour. Most other navies followed suit. The problem of concealment of merchant ships, which was of little consequence at this time, was left to be addressed at a later date when the need arose.

In October 1907, the Hague Peace Conference, expanding the provisions of the Geneva Convention, drew up further laws on the conduct of sea warfare and the rights of neutral nations and protected ships. Reversing, in part, the terms of the Declaration of Paris, which had sought to abolish the *guerre de course*, or commerce war, the use of AMCs and surface raiders was made internationally legitimate, reintroducing a form of privateering. However, under the terms of the agreement the approved vessels had to be listed as warships by the countries that operated them and they were required to fly the naval ensign. In consequence, the Conference also determined new prize rules that should be adopted by these vessels, as well as by submarines and other warships engaged in blockade or commerce war. The Conference laid down that any merchant vessel of either a belligerent or neutral power suspected of carrying contraband (*ie* war materials) should be visited and searched and, if she was found to be carrying contraband, adequate arrangements made for the safety of her crew and passengers before she could be captured or sunk.

In the event, during the two World Wars these regulations were often flagrantly ignored. They certainly did not provide secure grounds for re-evaluating the necessity for camouflage, as was made abundantly clear by the sinking of the *Lusitania* in May 1915 and the similar destruction of the *Athenia* in September 1939.

To afford some measure of protection to the merchant ships of non-belligerent nations, the Conference agreed the adoption of recognised hull marking procedures which would permit these vessels to display their neutral status and entitle them to dispensation from hostile action. The revisions and adaptations of the Geneva Convention that were made at the Hague Conference also finally established in full the conditions in which hospital ships would be entitled to immunity from attack during wartime. From this time all countries ratifying the agreement were required to nominate their hospital ships and register them, with a full description, with the International Red Cross, before placing them in service. They were also required to paint hospital ships in distinctive colours, according to their category, to facilitate their identification by hostile warships.

Three ships which were listed on the AMC register; Cunard's *Servia*... (*World Ship Photo Library*)

... Anchor Line's *City of Rome*, and ... (*CPL*)

... White Star Line's *Majestic*. (*CPL*)

Three more ships which were engaged in the Indian trooping service, P&O's *Dongola* of 1905, ... (*CPL*)

... British India Line's *Rewa* of 1906, and ... (*CPL*)

... the *Nubia* of 1895. (*CPL*)

The stipulated colouring in all cases was white hull and superstructure. Class 1 hospital ships (those permanently attached to the fleet in peacetime and those put into service by belligerents in wartime) were to have a 1½m-wide green band all round their hull, parallel to the waterline. Class 2 hospital ships (vessels furnished by the Red Cross Societies) and Class 3 hospital ships (vessels owned and equipped by neutral countries but chartered to a belligerent) were to have a 1½m-wide red band round their hull. In addition, all hospital ships were required to have red crosses painted on their hulls and funnels, which could be illuminated at night by some means, and to carry the Red Cross distinguishing flag on their ensign staff and main mast at all times. Their national flag was to be flown, as normal, on the jack staff.

From the end of the Second Boer War there was a respite from any major conflict involving the United Kingdom which lasted for 12 years but when World War I broke out in August 1914, trooping and other auxiliary duties commenced on an unprecedented scale. This new conflict extended geographically well beyond anything previously experienced and it was truly global in its nature. From the point of view of passenger shipping, virtually no commercial service was able to continue unaffected and the level of demand on the mercantile service to provide vessels for auxiliary employment in all categories remained undiminished for the next four years.

Theories on camouflage tactics now had the opportunity to be put into practical effect. What at the outset still amounted to little more than a precautionary measure, based on only the vaguest appreciation of the value of protective coloration, was, by the end of those four years, both a highly developed science and an ingenious art form.

World War I

DURING WORLD WAR I a further significant change in British trooping practice took place which severed the last direct links with the Royal Navy. This was the termination of total naval responsibility for trooping by the transfer of the transportation service to the newly created Sea Transport Section of the Ministry of Shipping in 1917. Requisitioned vessels were no longer under charter to the Admiralty, although the Admiralty retained responsibility for coordinating trooping operations with the ships of the Senior Service.

At the beginning of World War I there was a real hope, forlorn as it turned out, that an element of commercial sailings could continue unaffected in spite of the state of hostilities and, for a while at least, a number of passenger liners did continue about their regular schedules. The turning point was the sinking of the *Lusitania* and gradually thereafter more and more British and French vessels were either laid up or taken over for auxiliary employment. As far as possible, ships of neutral countries carried on regardless but being subject to the British blockade and in the face of the U-boat threat they were compelled to don the conspicuous displays of their identity as determined by the Hague Convention. These neutrality markings comprised the ship's name and/or nationality painted along both sides of the hull in large letters with the vessel's national flag, equally prominent, in the same vicinity.

British passenger ships found themselves being adapted to a number of auxiliary roles from the very outset. A sizeable group from the AMC register were provided with armaments and pressed into service as naval auxiliaries. The Navy formed the 10th Cruiser Squadron, otherwise known as Cruiser Force B, predominantly of such converted liners, many still manned by their brave civilian officers and crews as members of the Volunteer Reserve.

The 10th Cruiser Squadron was used to maintain the blockade of the North Sea, its patrol area extending from the Norwegian coast far out into the Atlantic and covering all approaches to the European continent from a northerly direction. In all, throughout the period of its existence, no fewer than forty-one different passenger ships served with the squadron for some length of time, each armed with guns up to 6in in calibre:

Alcantara	Royal Mail	*India*	P&O
Almanzora	Royal Mail	*Kildonan Castle*	Union Castle
Alsatian	Allan (flagship)	*Mantua*	P&O
Ambrose	Booth	*Moldavia*	P&O
Andes	Royal Mail	*Motagua*	Elders & Fyffes
Arlanza	Royal Mail	*Oceanic*	White Star
Armadale Castle	Union Castle	*Ophir*	Orient
Avenger (ex-*Aotearoa*)	Union SS Co NZ	*Orbita*	Pacific SN Co
Bayano	Elders & Fyffes	*Orcoma*	Pacific SN Co
Calyx (ex-*Calypso*)	Thomas Wilson	*Oropesa* (renamed *Champagne*)	Pacific SN Co
Caribbean	Royal Mail	*Orotava*	Pacific SN Co
Cedric	White Star	*Orvieto*	Orient
Changuinola	Elders & Fyffes	*Otway*	Pacific SN Co
Clan McNaughton	Clan	*Patia*	Elders & Fyffes
Columbella	Anchor	*Patnea*	Elders & Fyffes
Digby (renamed *Artois*)	Furness Warren	*Patuca*	Elders & Fyffes
Ebro	Royal Mail	*Teutonic*	White Star
Eskimo	Thomas Wilson	*Victorian*	Allan
Gloucestershire	Bibby	*Viknor* (ex-*Viking*)	Viking Cruising
Hilary	Booth	*Virginian*	Allan
Hildebrand	Booth		

Among the countries whose ships displayed neutrality markings in World War I were Denmark, the Netherlands, Spain and the USA. Shown here are the DFDS ships *Oscar II*… (*World Ship Photo Library*)

… and *Frederick VIII.* (Tom Rayner)

Banana boats at war. Elders & Fyffes *Changuinola* auxiliary cruiser with the 10th Cruiser Squadron, and… (*Imperial War Museum*)

... the second *Bayano*, convoy escort vessel. (*Tom Rayner*)

Apart from the 10th Cruiser Squadron many other passenger ships were also converted to AMCs to relieve the strain on the Navy's regular cruisers by undertaking lone patrol and, later, convoy escort duties. However, experience with bigger vessels such as the *Aquitania* and *Mauretania* showed them to be unsuitable for this work, owing to their size. Though she was converted into an AMC, the *Mauretania* was not, in the event, commissioned, while the *Aquitania* was actually in service for only two weeks. On 22 August 1914 she collided with the Leyland Line's steamer *Canadian* and, although she

Flagship of the 10th Cruiser Squadron, the *Alsatian* in dazzle colours. (*Tom Rayner*)

Royal Holland Lloyd's *Gelria* in neutrality markings which identify her port of registry rather than her country of ownership. (*Imperial War Museum*)

was returned to Liverpool for repairs, she did not resume AMC duties on their completion.

The two other large Atlantic express liners, the *Olympic* and *Lusitania*, were also intended for conversion to AMC but, for the same reason, were never taken in hand. Unfortunately, the *Lusitania*'s presence on the AMC register may have had an indirect bearing on her sinking. In spite of the accusations and recriminations following her destruction, which were hardly appeased by the Germans' indifferent attitude to the gravity of their deed, there was some credibility in the German suspicion that the *Lusitania* may have been armed and modified while at sea in the same way that they had

The *Lusitania* sinking by the head off the Old Head of Kinsale on 7 May 1915, as depicted in a painting by Norman Wilkinson from the *Illustrated London News* of 15 May 1915. The original caption described the torpedo attack as an act of 'wilful and wholesale murder'. (*Illustrated London News*)

Norddeutscher Lloyd's *Kaiser Wilhelm der Grosse*, blackened for her brief career as a commerce raider. (*WZ-Bildienst*)

done with many of their own liners. The fact that the *Lusitania* was still wearing her Cunard colours does not discredit this claim for both the *Aquitania* and *Mauretania* retained their commercial livery as AMCs, as photographs clearly demonstrate.

The French also introduced AMCs into their surface fleet but the Germans preferred instead to utilise their large and fast express steamers as commerce raiders to harass the Allies' supply lines. On the outbreak of war they had some forty-two ships designated for this role dispersed at various locations around the world.

With their unlikely background and their special rules of engagement, armed passenger liners acquired a kind of gladiatorial or buccaneering image with the general public. Their dramatic exploits caught the imagination and were widely and vividly reported in whatever war news was permitted to be released on the home front. These activities featured particularly prominently in the early months of the war as a result of a series of notorious engagements which only enhanced this popular view of these ships.

Disguise was a ploy adopted by many of the vessels involved in these combat actions, this being a method of deception that both sides readily exploited.

Norddeutscher Lloyd's first Atlantic Blue Riband holder, the *Kaiser Wilhelm der Grosse*, was painted all black as a concealment measure, fitted with guns and sent secretly to sea with orders to attack or capture as many British merchant vessels as possible. It is hard to see how being darkened in this fashion would in any way have made her less conspicuous, for she had a distinctive and easily recognised profile with her four funnels arranged in pairs. Besides, darker ships tended to stand out more against the horizon than those painted in lighter tones, especially at night, although it is only fair to say that at the outset of World War I many British troopships were similarly painted either all dark grey or black.

After sinking some 10,500 gross tons of shipping and gallantly allowing two ships, the *Galician* and the *Arlanza*, to proceed unharmed because they were carrying passengers, the *Kaiser Wilhelm der Grosse* was finally cornered when depleted coal stocks forced her into Rio de Oro, Spanish West Africa, to replenish. This single incident graphically

***Kaiser Wilhelm der Grosse* sunk following the action with HMS *High Flyer* on 26 August 1914. (*L L von Münching*)**

Two of the large, shortlived armed merchant cruisers, the *Aquitania* and ... (*Imperial War Museum*)

... *Mauretania*. Note their gun mountings aft and that both vessels are still painted in their civilian colourings. (*Imperial War Museum*)

demonstrated the vulnerability of employing these large, fast liners as auxiliary cruisers. Their enormous fuel consumption, combined with the logistical problems involved in providing discrete but ample bunkering facilities in remote places, rendered their operation unviable. While refuelling, the *Kaiser Wilhelm der Grosse* was disturbed by the cruiser HMS *Highflyer*, which had been tipped off as to the liner's whereabouts, and on 26 August 1914, following a brief exchange of fire, she was sunk.

The *Kaiser Wilhelm der Grosse*'s fleetmate, the *Kronprinz Wilhelm*, performed a similar role, though she was repainted grey, until exhausted fuel supplies forced her to run the British blockade of the American coast on 10 April 1915. Of the other ships of Norddeutscher Lloyd's record-breaking quartet, the *Kaiser Wilhelm II* was interned in the United States from the very beginning of the war while her sister, the *Kronprinzessin Cecilie*, made a particularly audacious escape into these same, then neutral, waters only days after the commencement of hostilities. This was achieved in part by her being disguised as the White Star liner *Olympic*. Four days out from New York when war broke

The German auxiliary cruiser *Kronprinz Wilhelm*. (*Imperial War Museum*)

Sailors repainting the *Kronprinzessin Cecilie*'s funnels while she was underway. (*Author's collection*)

The *Kronprinzessin Cecilie* anchored outside Bar Harbor, Maine on 4 August 1914, disguised as the White Star Liner *Olympic*. (*Frank Braynard*)

out, she was carrying a consignment of gold bullion which her master was anxious should not fall into British hands. To prevent this from happening, he elected to turn his ship about and seek refuge in a neutral United States port. Knowing that British warships had already been stationed along the perimeter of American territorial waters, something needed to be done to the ship's appearance to give him the extra breathing space that would increase his chances of breaking through. So while the ship was steaming full ahead, seamen were hoisted on bosun's chairs around her scorching funnels to paint their tops black in the style of the White Star Line. Whether it would have worked or not we shall never know. Steaming flat out for the American coast and conveniently hidden in a protective blanket of thick fog she was able to reach the safety of Bar Harbor, Maine, without having to put her disguise to the test. The *Kronprinzessin Cecilie* remained at Bar Harbor until the following spring when she was escorted to Boston for internment. In 1917 she was taken over as an American troopship under the name *Mount Vernon*, but by then she was but a shadow of her former glory and her infantry passengers nicknamed her 'Mount Vermin' for obvious reasons.

Disguise was a favourite ruse of the Germans and it was an artifice they used to good effect in both World Wars. At best it could permit complete freedom from interference, at worst it could cause sufficient confusion to gain valuable time for retreat or to initiate some other defensive manoeuvre. Thanks in part to such changes to their identity, a number of other German passenger vessels rearmed for raider duties during World War I were able to slip into the Atlantic without being intercepted. Norddeutscher Lloyd's *Berlin*, which was also disguised as a British ship, managed to elude the blockade of the North Sea, taking with her a quantity of mines which were used most profitably. One was struck by the battleship HMS *Audacious* on 27 October 1914 causing her to sink in spite of a valiant effort by the *Olympic* to tow her to port. Other German auxiliaries masqueraded as the vessels of neutral Scandinavian companies, repainted and renamed accordingly. Some were caught but many got through.

Another form of disguise altogether was adopted by the Hamburg Sud-Amerika liner *Cap Trafalgar*. Barely three weeks after the sinking of the *Kaiser Wilhelm der Grosse*, she was involved in action with the AMC *Carmania* which, ironically, was also disguised.

Having received her orders at Buenos Aires, the *Cap Trafalgar* coaled at Montevideo and then rendezvoused off Bahia Blanca with the gunboat *Eber* which transferred weapons and other equipment to her. On 13 September 1914, off the Brazilian island of Trinidada, she was interrupted in the act of coaling by the *Carmania*. After a brief period of uncertainty as to the identity of their opponents, a fierce battle ensued, the British vessel emerging victorious from this classic encounter. The clash was both the first and last to take place between opposing passenger liners.

The recognition problem that had been initially experienced resulted from the effective application of a measure of deception by both ships. The *Cap Trafalgar*'s engineers had removed her third (dummy) funnel and added mock bridge wings to her sides. While tactically the alterations produced the desired effect, so that the British officers were quite unsure of the identity of the ship they were challenging, strategically they cost her dear. The sacrificed funnel had also housed condensers feeding the ship's boilers. Their removal necessitated the shut-down of one engine, robbing her of almost two knots' speed, a critical loss for she was already marginally the slower vessel. But if her exterior modifications had bemused those aboard the *Carmania*, so too had the alterations to the British ship puzzled the Germans. The *Carmania*'s master had considered his ship to be too readily recognisable as a British vessel. Her carpenter was consequently charged with knocking up a dummy third funnel out of wood and canvas. The well-known painting of the duel between the *Carmania* and the *Cap Trafalgar* does not show the Cunard ship with this addition to her profile, perhaps because it was destroyed early on. After nearly two hours of intense action the *Cap Trafalgar* capsized onto her port side and sank bow first, while the extensively damaged and incapacitated *Carmania* required assistance to

For comparison, a peacetime view of the *Olympic*, showing her during her one and only visit to Liverpool on 1 June 1911. (*Tom Rayner*)

Cunard Line's *Carmania* seen during peacetime. (*John Clarkson*)

HMS *Carmania* and the *Cap Trafalgar* in the thick of their duel on 14 September 1914. The painting by Charles Dixon comes from a commemorative booklet. (*University of Liverpool, Cunard archives*)

reach port. That December another British AMC triumphed when, with HMS *Bristol*, P&O's *Macedonia* despatched Admiral Von Spee's supply ships *Baden* and *Santa Isabel* during the Battle of the Falklands.

The alteration of ships' silhouettes to render them unrecognisable, a tactic known as dynamic camouflage, was another technique widely used by the combatants of both World Wars. Apart from the addition or subtraction of funnels, a particularly ingenious trick was to create the effect of a symmetrical, double-ended vessel, with navigation bridges and

The *Vineta* (ex-*Cap Polonio*) with one funnel removed prior to commencement of her planned career as an auxiliary cruiser. She provides an impression of the disguised appearance of her Hamburg Sud fleetmate *Cap Trafalgar*, except that the *Cap Trafalgar* had her funnels repainted in the colours of the Union Castle Line. (*Arnold Kludas*)

HMS *Macedonia*, Armed Merchant Cruiser, seen painted in two tone grey in April 1918. (*Imperial War Museum*)

The *Dunvegan Castle* and ... (*World Ship Photo Library*)

... *Norman* conveyed the first units of the British Expeditionary Force to Europe in 1914. (*Real Photos*)

suitably inclined masts at each end, so that an observer might also be confused as to the ship's direction.

At the beginning of World War I the movement of troops was the other primary function of requisitioned passenger liners, the initial task being the conveyance of the British Expeditionary Force from Southampton to Belgium. The first sailings were made by the Union Castle Line ships *Dunvegan Castle* and *Norman*. Painted all grey by this time, many of these same vessels were also employed to transport Empire fighting units to the European war zones and later to the Dardanelles for the ill-fated Gallipoli offensive.

The *Mauretania*, darkened, at Mudros. In the foreground, men from HMS *Lord Nelson* freshen up with a bathe in the sea. (*Imperial War Museum*)

The Dardanelles campaign saw the big liners called up for troop carrying. The *Olympic*, at Mudros, now darkened overall, is interestingly displaying two numbers – 267 on her side and 2810 just below the bridge. (*Imperial War Museum*)

Liners as battleships and battlecruisers – the *Oruba* as HMS *Orion*. She was later sunk deliberately at Kephalos to form a breakwater against the fierce northwesterly gales. (*Imperial War Museum*)

IT WOULD BE REMISS not to mention a most unusual exercise in dynamic deception which involved a special group of British liners early in World War I. What made this particular scheme so peculiar was not so much the technicalities of the disguises (although they were bizarre enough) as the objectives behind their application. Reversing the principle of the Q-ships, in which apparently innocent cargo vessels, with guns stowed beneath boats and in holds, acted as submarine lures, the Admiralty contrived to give the enemy the impression that these vulnerable, unarmoured merchant vessels were actually powerful, threatening machines of war – paper tigers, no less!

Fourteen ships in total were selected for the task, each remodelled individually with mock turrets, guns and other sham devices made of wood and canvas, and specially ballasted, to enable them to masquerade as the capital ships of the Grand Fleet. They were:

City of Oxford (Ellerman)	as HMS *St Vincent*
Michigan (Warren)	as HMS *Collingwood*
Montezuma (Canadian Pacific)	as HMS *Iron Duke*
Ruthenia (Canadian Pacific)	as HMS *King George V*
Tyrolia (Canadian Pacific)	as HMS *Centurion*
Oruba (Orient)	as HMS *Orion*
Mount Royal (Canadian Pacific)	as HMS *Marlborough*
Montcalm (Candian Pacific)	as HMS *Audacious*
Princess (ex-*Kronprinzessin Cecilie*) (Hamburg Amerika)	as HMS *Ajax*
Perthshire (Federal SN)	as HMS *Vanguard*
Cevic (White Star)	as HMS *Queen Mary*
Manipur (Brocklebank)	as HMS *Indomitable*
Patrician (Harrison)	as HMS *Invincible*
Merion (American)	as HMS *Tiger*

Apart from certain conversions of passenger liners into aircraft carriers, of which more will be said later, these disguises resulted in the most extreme vicissitudes to appearance ever known for ships of this type. Just how successful these dummy battleships and battlecruisers were is not known. The objective behind the subterfuge was to confuse the enemy over fleet dispositions, but it had the advantage that the Germans might also be misled into believing that Britain's naval strength was greater than it actually was. It is a sobering thought, however, that for the operation to have had maximum beneficial effect the merchant decoys were presumably regarded as expendable. However, apart from the *Merion*, which was sunk in the Aegean Sea by UB8 on 30 May 1915, all survived. By the beginning of 1916 two of the remaining vessels had been expended as blockships and the others were diverted to other duties.

During World War II a similar decoy conversion exercise was implemented, though on a much smaller scale. In this instance a pair of old merchant vessels were done up as dummy *King George V* class battleships and stationed at Rosyth deliberately to fool the Luftwaffe.

Dummy battleship HMS *Centurion* (ex-*Tyrolia*). (*Imperial War Museum*)

For comparison, the real thing, the battleship HMS *Orion*. (*Imperial War Museum*)

The *Merion*, the dummy *Tiger*, had been present in the Aegean in support of the Allies' Dardanelles campaign. In April 1915, Britain and France invaded the Gallipoli peninsula in a bid to force a supply route through to Russia via the Bosphorus and the Black Sea. It was hoped, simultaneously, to gain the allegiance of the Balkan States. In the event, the whole operation proved a costly disaster, both in the failure to achieve the initial objective and because Bulgaria ended up joining the side of the Central Powers – Germany, Austro-Hungary and Turkey. In terms of casualties, the overflowing hospitals in Malta and Alexandria testified to the vast numbers inflicted.

The island of Lemnos was made the combined headquarters in the battle zone, with its harbour at Mudros the main disembarkation port. From Mudros the soldiers were carried up to the battle front aboard the Cunarder *Franconia* and the same ship was also used for carrying back the wounded for onwards transportation to military hospitals. Within a year many of the liners bringing in troops were, like the *Franconia*, carrying out casualties after conversion into hospital ships.

A total of twenty-two British or Empire merchant vessels were employed as hospital ships at some time during the Gallipoli campaign, among them the three 'great liners', the *Aquitania*, *Britannic* and *Mauretania*. The *Aquitania* was, in fact, the longest serving of these big Dardanelles hospital ships, continuing in this role until December 1917. The French also contributed many of their former passenger liners for conversion to hospital ships, CGT's trans-Atlantic flagship *France* being notable among them.

Unlike these ships, which were entitled to protection from attack under the Geneva Convention, the *Franconia* and nineteen other vessels like her were classed as ambulance transports or 'black hospital ships'. These were also equipped to convey and treat sick and wounded but they doubled as troop and stores carriers on return voyages

American Line's *Merion* as the battlecruiser HMS *Tiger* and ... **(*Imperial War Museum*)**

... the *Merion* prior to conversion, for comparison. **(*World Ship Photo Library*)**

to battle areas. They acquired their sobriquet because, unlike the regular hospital ships, they did not wear the distinguishing Red Cross colours and consequently were unable to claim protection under the Geneva Convention.

A third type of hospital ship was the hospital carrier. These vessels also wore the regulation hospital ship colours and were protected under the Geneva Convention, but they were not fully fitted out with wards, surgery, dispensary and so on. Outwardly they could not be distinguished from full hospital ships and ultimately many were completely converted.

When studying photographs, it is interesting to note, considering the quite specific terms of the colouring regulations for hospital ships, that there was considerable variation in the interpretation of these rules. Not all British ships, for instance, displayed the Red Cross symbol on their funnels, which were painted in a buff shade rather than white.

By Autumn 1915, it was both realised and accepted that the Dardanelles offensive had

The 'great liner' hospital ships – the *Aquitania* departing Southampton, assisted by tugs. (*Imperial War Museum*)

Following her period of service as a troopship, the *Mauretania* was repainted in hospital ship colours in September 1915. (*CPL*)

Cunard Line's *Franconia* was the principal ambulance transport during the Dardanelles Campaign. (*CPL*)

A view of the *Aquitania* showing her with rather dirty paintwork near the end of her hospital ship career. (*Imperial War Museum*)

The *Mauretania*. Note how her hull band does not extend around her stern, whereas that of ... (*Imperial War Museum*)

... the *Britannic*, also seen here leaving Southampton, continues right around her hull. (*Imperial War Museum*)

The *Britannic*'s hospital ship colours are clearly shown in this view. See the Red Cross flag flying from her foremast. (*A Duncan*)

The French hospital ships *France IV* and ... (*Cie Générale Maritime*)

... *Lafayette* both served at the Dardanelles. The *Lafayette* is seen here at Bordeaux in 1917 prior to departure for Salonica. (*Cie Générale Maritime*)

The hospital ship *Devanha* at Mudros. (*CPL*)

totally failed and, when Bulgaria overran Serbia and Montenegro that October, the invasion force was withdrawn. Like Dunkirk, twenty-five years later, the evacuation operation, which took from November 1915 to February of the following year, was a complete success but it left the Allies with little more than a toehold in this important region, with the British garrison at Salonika. Again, converted passenger liners excelled themselves, working round the clock, often close in shore and continuously exposed to the risks of mine and torpedo.

P&O Line's *Egypt*. After World War I she was sunk in collision off the coast of France and achieved fame in a spectacular salvage operation during which $5 million worth of gold and a similar value of bank notes were recovered from her wreck. (*CPL*)

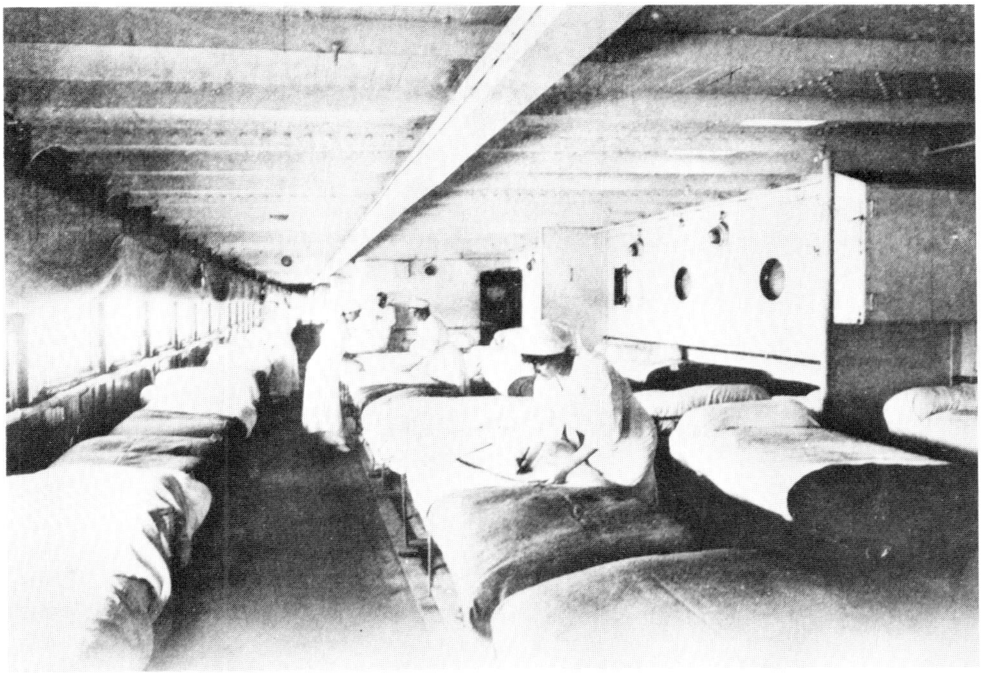

This scene aboard the *France IV* gives a good impression of the cramped conditions, with so many casualties, even on such a big ship measuring 23,666 gross tons. (*Cie Générale Maritime*)

By the time the withdrawal from Gallipoli was nearing completion, mercantile losses in both the Mediterranean and Atlantic were reaching alarming proportions. For the U-boat commanders this was the high point of their offensive and it would be fair to say that their actions alone threatened the direst of consequences for the Allies unless the trend could be reversed. The cost of the war was by then threatening Britain with bankruptcy and

Some smaller World War I hospital ships – the *Ebani*, with hull stripe and colours generally faded and in need of a fresh coat of paint. (*Tom Rayner*)

During World War I the peacetime troopship *Assaye* was converted into a hospital ship, as were her sister ships *Plassy* and *Sobraon*. (*CPL*)

she could ill afford this punishing attrition to vital supplies. Worse was to come, however, for the Central Powers declared their intention to wage unrestricted submarine warfare from 1 February 1917, abrogating the Geneva Convention and rendering all vessels of protected categories legitimate targets. With the Allies' lifeline of food and armaments at risk from being cut off, the Atlantic Ocean, and the Western Approaches in particular, became a new battle front demanding special tactics and weapons in the savage war being waged on its grey expanse. The Allies urgently needed to implement measures that would turn the tide of fortune in their favour, and in naval circles it was a problem of which all ranks were acutely aware.

The *Saint Margaret of Scotland*, converted from the Royal Mail passenger ship *Balantia* in 1916. (*Tom Rayner*)

The *Wandilla* of the Adelaide Steamship Company, identification number C6801. (*Tom Rayner*)

The *Nevasa*, former Admiralty peacetime troopship. Compare this photograph with the picture on page 26. (*World Ship Photo Library*)

It was at this point that Lieutenant Norman Wilkinson RNVR, the already famous marine artist, appeared on the scene. Like many of his creative contemporaries, who were conscious of the dilemma confronting the Allies, he advanced revolutionary ideas on how he considered the whole approach to applying protective colouring might be modified to more beneficial effect. His carefully detailed proposals were submitted to Captain Charles Thorpe, Flag Captain, Devonport on 27 April 1917.

It was not the first time that a prominent artist had made suggestions about camouflage techniques. Back in 1899, the American painter George DeForest Brush, who was known for his studies of protective coloration in nature, propounded a camouflage scheme that was intended to reduce the undesirable visibility levels that resulted from the standard United States Navy colour systems of that time. It is interesting to note that from November 1913 the British Press had been advocating the adoption, by the Admiralty, of the 'Brush' low visibility painting method for British ships too, albeit without success.

Wilkinson's theories were considerably more radical than Brush's, however, and it is a tribute to the open-mindedness of the Admiralty of the day and, perhaps, a measure of the desperate crisis confronting the nation, that their response was both positive and encouraging. Arrangements were made to give Wilkinson all the help he needed to implement and evaluate his scheme and for this purpose the storeship *Industry* was made available for experimental repainting.

The principle behind Norman Wilkinson's proposed scheme, based on conclusions drawn from his own observations of darkly painted transports, which made rather easy targets, was that it was virtually impossible to render ships either invisible or indistinct because, when viewed from a submarine's periscope they were seen not against a sea background but against the sky at the horizon. If this premise was accepted, then the only logical alternative was to attempt to break up a ship's outline so as to make identification and judgement of size more difficult. More importantly, it would make the range and direction of a target harder to determine and so confuse a U-boat that he would adopt the wrong firing position when he released his torpedoes. In this respect, it should be remembered that such decisions often had to be made hastily, in conditions in which the target was frequently obscured by the motion of the waves.

Such a scheme clearly could not be described as camouflage, however, for strictly speaking that was not the intention in this case. The term camouflage is derived from the

The *Caronia*, sister ship to the victor of the *Carmania/Cap Trafalgar* duel, seen in convoy sporting a dazzle colour scheme consisting of stripes, blocks and patches. (*Tom Rayner*)

The Orient Liner *Ormonde* in a distinctive multi-coloured scheme based on an angular design. (*P&O*)

Red Star Line's *Lapland* in a striped dazzle livery. The lighter stripes on the sides of her bow reveal the strong contrast in both the colours and tones used on her. (*Author's collection*)

French verb *camoufler* (to disguise) and is generally regarded as meaning to conceal or obscure, both objectives being the complete reverse of what was intended by Norman Wilkinson. Hence the term dazzle painting was ascribed to this method of deceptive colouring. Later, as the technique was developed, these schemes came to be known as Disruptive Patterns in Admiralty circles, and as Confusion or Pattern Systems by the United States Navy.

A Dazzle Section was set up by the Admiralty within the Directorate of Naval Equipment. It was placed under the supervision of Wilkinson, now promoted to Lieutenant Commander, and, after some deliberation, the Section was established at Burlington House, the home of the Royal Academy of Arts. This immediate association with a centre of fine art is interesting for it set the pattern for both the Dazzle Section staffing composition and its approach to the task. Wilkinson assembled around him a group of accomplished artists, all of whom were given commissions as Lieutenant RNVR: Leonard Campbell-Taylor, Christopher Clark, Montague Dawson, John Gregory, Bryan Hook, Cecil Charles King, Frank H Mason, J C Mottram, A O'Connell, Julius Olsson,

The *Belgic* was one of a number of liners which had their construction interrupted by the war but which were hurriedly completed to serve as emergency troop/cargo ships. Others included the *Orca* and *Minnekahda*. After the war the *Belgic* was rebuilt emerging as originally intended as the three-funnelled *Belgenland*. (*Tom Rayner*)

Applying the dazzle colouring patterns to each ship presented quite a challenge due to the vast differences in scale between plan and the real thing. Painters are here seen applying dazzle colours to the port side of the *Olympic*. (*Illustrated London News*)

The finished result. The *Olympic* being towed from dock, displaying for the first time her initial dazzle colour scheme. (*Illustrated London News*)

In order to fox the U-boats it was necessary at intervals to make changes to dazzle patterns. Here the *Olympic* shows off her second scheme, seen here from the port bow quarter … (*Imperial War Museum*)

… and here from the port stern quarter. Later, this disguise was modified further. The stripes across her bow were removed while four oval shapes were painted on her port side between the first and second funnels. The starboard side pattern was also changed. (*Imperial War Museum*)

Staying with the *Olympic*, this stern aerial view shows clearly how dazzle colour schemes extended right over ships, being taken round funnels, masts and ventilators, and even over lifeboats. (*L L von Münching*)

Steven Spurrier, Gordon Stevenson, Edward Wadsworth, Frederic Waugh and Hubert Alington Yockney.

Edward Wadsworth was well known as a leading member of the Vorticist movement, a group of abstract painters, engravers and sculptors whose work derived its inspiration from the mechanics and driving forces of industrial society. This was particularly pertinent to the work of the Dazzle Section, in which the vast steel hulls of ships became the canvases upon which the artists created their bizarre, modernist patterns.

Within a very short while the dazzle team comprised, apart from the fifteen artists, three modellers and eleven female painters whose job was to colour ships' plans. Ten of the artists were stationed at ports around the country where the ships were painted and the remainder worked at Burlington House with Wilkinson and his assistant, King. Initially, the work involved considerable experimentation and assimilation of the feedback from the *Industry* trial. After completion of her repainting she had undertaken a coastwise voyage so that observations and assessments could be made. The majority of these were favourable. To gauge the impact of different patterns and to develop designs suitable for particular types of vessel, a great deal of work had to be done making and painting models. These were then observed, using a periscope device, in a viewing theatre (described in Appendix 4) specially constructed by Norman Wilkinson and Cecil King.

It was important to ensure that dazzle schemes should not provide, inadvertently, the means by which the enemy could identify individual ships. For maximum effectiveness, therefore, the patterns were made different on each side of the hull and certain key vessels had their overall colour scheme modified at intervals or changed completely. A good example of this is the *Olympic* which, as photographs reveal, had her dazzle scheme altered at least twice.

Typical dazzle designs for given classes of ship, contrived at Burlington House, were sent to the officers on location, two of which were stationed in the Port of London and one each at Southampton, Newcastle, Humberside, Glasgow, Liverpool, Bristol, Cardiff and Belfast. These officers then adapted the typical design to suit each ship and in this they were more or less given a completely free hand. It was especially important, in doing this, for them to consider the relative areas of contrasting paint in each scheme. If the painted areas were too large, the shape of the ship would reveal itself: if they were too small the scheme would loose its effectiveness to confuse at a distance.

The Dazzle Section's first task was the repainting of fifty troopships but in a very short time the number of dazzled vessels of all types could be counted in hundreds. Britain's allies took an immediate interest in the extraordinary colour schemes being applied to her auxiliaries, cargo ships and, ultimately, her warships and following visits to the Dazzle Section by representatives of the French, Italian and Japanese Governments, these countries also adopted the dazzle system of protective colouring. Early in 1918 Norman Wilkinson was invited to visit the United States to advise the Navy Department on the intricacies of designing and applying deceptive colouring to both merchant ships and warships.

There was considerable variety to the patterns employed in dazzle painting: the *Mauretania* was probably unique in having a chequer-board type scheme which was similar on both sides of the hull. The colours used included greys, blues and vivid reds. (*Tom Rayner*)

This scheme applied to the *Melita* features characteristic patches of dark colours with lighter shades. (*CPL*)

ON 6 APRIL 1917 the United States had entered the war on the side of the Allies; a welcome relief, for the young American infantrymen brought a fresh vitality to the tired batallions bogged down in the Flanders mud. Transporting these troops to Europe was a major undertaking requiring a vast fleet of ships. All the interned German liners were seized and adapted for this purpose but, with their British and French counterparts, they presented a prime target for the waiting U-boats.

Thus, following America's entry into the conflict, action on camouflage matters was spurred on and, quite separate from the initiative involving Norman Wilkinson, the Submarine Defense Association's Engineering Committee sponsored the establishment of a special department dedicated to camouflage research. The Association had been established by, and represented the interests of, nearly a hundred leading American and British shipping, export and marine insurance companies. It perceived camouflage as a relatively new and unreliable practice and was concerned about the lack of scientific standards in the application of protective measures and the apparent absence of any understanding of how these paint changes could contribute to the obfuscation of targeted ships. The Eastman Kodak Company was approached to see if they would agree to

Nelson Line's *Highland Rover* displaying a dazzle colour scheme which, in black and white, hints at the disruptive systems that were to be adopted during World War II. (*CPL*)

Striped dazzle patterns were particularly popular as the selection here demonstrates: the *Empress of Russia*. (*Canadian Pacific*)

The *Field Marshall*, formerly the Deutsche Ost Afrika Line's *Feldmarschall*, with stripes fore and aft and plain paint in between. (*Tom Rayner*)

The *Aquitania* swopped her hospital ship dress for this dazzle scheme which is distinguished by bold serrations. Compare this photograph with that of the *Leviathan*, on page 74, whose camouflage design also featured saw tooth patterns. (*Imperial War Museum*)

Royal Holland Lloyd's *Zealandia* in an intensely striped colour scheme. (*Tom Rayner*)

The Union Castle Line ship *Walmer Castle* is painted in the same scheme as the *Empress of Russia*, demonstrating that dazzle patterns were not exclusive to each ship. The basic patterns were widely applied but often adapted in individual cases to enhance the desired effect. (*Tom Rayner*)

A poor photograph of the *Walmer Castle* which shows how her dazzle design, compared with the previous photograph, was substantially altered. It is not known which of the two schemes was the earlier. (*Real Photos*)

The *Ulimaroa*'s dazzle scheme is less geometric in style and resembles the American Warner camouflage system as painted on the *Orizaba* and *Siboney*, page 71; and *Agamemnon*, page 70. (*Tom Rayner*)

The *Balmoral Castle* also sports a camouflage pattern similar to the system developed for American vessels by Everett L Warner. (*Tom Rayner*)

This dazzle scheme on the Federal Steam Navigation Company's *Argyllshire* mixes stripes with patches of solid colour. (*Imperial War Museum*)

The *Argus* was an early conversion of a passenger ship into an aircraft carrier, having been reconstructed from the incomplete Italian liner *Conte Rosso*. These vessels were also given dazzle colours. (*Imperial War Museum*)

This rather poor picture of the French liner *France* in dazzle livery is interesting as it demonstrates one of the popular subterfuges of painted camouflage. By deliberately emphasising the contrast between dark and light colours on her funnels, the three light funnels forward tend to disappear and she is seen, from a distance, as a single-funnelled ship. In the case of the *France* the aftermost funnel was darkened. On the similarly painted *Mount Vernon* (ex-*Kronprinzessin Cecilie*), the forward most of the four funnels was darkened. (*Cie Générale Maritime*)

undertake the necessary investigations, a move which was approved by US Navy Secretary, Josephus Daniels. A branch of the Maintenance Division of the Navy's Bureau of Construction and Repair was therefore established in the Physics Department of the Eastman Kodak Research Laboratories at Rochester, New York, on 15 March 1918. Dr C E Kenneth Mees, Head of the Research Laboratories, stipulated that a Kodak person should be in charge of the new section and nominated Loyd Ancile Jones, a distinguished physicist, for the post. The Navy Secretary agreed this appointment and Jones was commissioned as a Lieutenant in the US Navy Reserve.

Hence, the American approach, in marked contrast to the British, was distinctly and predominantly scientific, although one artist, John Bettinger, was attached to the Kodak team. Also, as in Britain, several prominent artists had offered suggestions to both the Navy Department and the US Shipping Board on possible camouflage techniques and of these proposals, seven were recognised and approved by the Camouflage Section for immediate application, pending the results of formal studies.

When America entered World War I her transports were also painted initially in navy grey. Here the *George Washington* leads the *America* and *De Kalb* (ex-*Prinz Eitel Friedrich*) in convoy. (*Imperial War Museum*)

Another former German liner in grey livery – the *Von Steuben* (ex-*Kronprinz Wilhelm*) at Brest. (*Imperial War Museum*)

Troops aboard the *Mount Vernon* (ex-*Kronprinzessin Cecile*), a view in early 1918 before her funnels were repainted. (*Imperial War Museum*)

The Warner disruptive colour scheme is clearly displayed in this view of the *Agamemnon* (ex-*Kaiser Wilhelm II*). (*Imperial War Museum*)

The *Orizaba* seen broadside on ... (*United States National Archives*)

... and the *Siboney*, Ward Line sisters, are also shown wearing the Warner design of disruptive camouflage. (*United States National Archives*)

The Mackay disruptive low visibility scheme is displayed here by the *De Kalb* (ex *Prinz Eitel Friedrich*), a former German Liner seized by the US Government on 6 October 1917. (*United States Naval Historical Center*)

The *Louisville* (ex-*St Louis*) painted in Mackay low visibility colours, like her sister *Knoxville* (ex *St Paul*), prior to capsizing in New York on 25 April 1918. (*United States National Archives*)

Later, the *Louisville* was repainted in dazzle colours. (*United States Naval Historial Center*)

They included low visibility schemes by William Andrew Mackay, a New York painter and illustrator, and George DeForest Brush. Brush's low visibility method was derived from Abbott Henderson Thayer's Law of Counter-Shading. It sought to eliminate or diminish the tendency of light to emphasise the three-dimensional depth of deck structures by painting exposed, light-facing surfaces darker, while shaded surfaces were made lighter.

In contrast, the approach to low visibility advocated by Mackay was much more complex. Mackay had undertaken detailed investigation of the structure of light and of the visible spectrum. He had developed his camouflage theories very much as a scientist rather than as an artist, exploiting the principles by which the human eye synthesises colour.

Colour vision is a product of the mind's response to varying wavelengths of light energy, rather than a property of objects themselves. White light is made up of the colours of the spectrum, as a rainbow or prism will reveal, each colour corresponding to a different wavelength of vibrating, radiating electromagnetic energy. The retina of the eye contains sensory, cone-shaped receptors for colour vision which can only be stimulated by light energy of the three primary wavelengths – red, green and violet/blue. The full range of colours that it is possible to perceive results from the additive process of mixing light of these primary colours in varying ratios or by diluting light from a single primary colour with light of all three primary wavelengths, that is with white light.

For his low visibility colouring system, Mackay undertook the spectrum analysis of the light radiating from the sea with a view to synthesising these same colours on ships' sides

The *Orizaba* seen from the port bow. (*United States National Archives*)

in a stipple effect that the eye would have difficulty resolving at a distance. His experiments led him to various blends of the primary colours that synthesised greys, blues and greens, and these were applied on hulls in a pattern that matched the variation of the colour of the water from that immediately around a ship to that of the distant horizon.

Though Mackay's system was ambitious and could not cope with drastic changes in light level which could significantly affect the appearance of the sea, it was, nevertheless, fairly successful. More importantly, it represented one of the earliest attempts to devise a system of camouflage through the recognition and control of the fundamental principles of vision. After the war, William Andrew Mackay became director of the US Navy's Camouflage Training School in New York.

Besides the low visibility measures officially endorsed by the Eastman Kodak Camouflage Research Center, a pseudo-dazzle scheme was offered by the landscape painter and water colour artist, Everett Langley Warner, who is credited as being the first camouflage artist to have declared that simulating invisibility was practically impossible and that effort should be concentrated instead on making ships unrecognisable. Another dazzle-type system was proposed by Watson, a skilled painter employed in the Norfolk Navy Yard, but this was applied only to warships.

Between these extremes were three further colouring techniques which aimed both to create a degree of concealment at long ranges and to cause confusion at short ranges. One of these hybrid schemes, which were the forerunners of the disruption systems of World War II, also came from William Andrew Mackay. The others were contrived by the artists Maximilian Toch and Lewis E Herzog. The Submarine Defense Association also devised a low visibility deception scheme, employing stripes, patches and chequered areas in greys and blues, but this was not adopted. Interestingly, the Submarine Defense Association also made other recommendations for aiding concealment and confusion including the use of smokeless fuels, the erection on deck of canvas or metal screens and the removal, shortening or repositioning of masts.

Thereafter the main thrust of American camouflage activity continued to be scientific for, as Loyd Jones stated later, 'Some means of measurement was highly desirable in order that the claims of the various systems might be correctly evaluated by a method not involving personal judgement'. At that time no method was available for the numerical specification of visibility, nor was there any instrument for its quantitative measurement.

The *Leviathan* (ex-*Vaterland*) commenced troop carrying duties painted in standard navy grey. From 1918 she appeared in this Admiralty derived dazzle design. Other American ships benefited from Admiralty schemes but ultimately the US Navy developed its own, very similar, dazzle camouflage system. (*United States National Archives*)

Jones set for his team the objectives of determining these fundamental principles and inventing, as appropriate, special instruments which could be used to calculate comparative values. Much of the team's time was also occupied with investigating the process of vision, for it was considered that a deeper appreciation of this phenomenon could also assist in the development of more effective camouflage by exploiting the means by which the vision process might be deceived.

Vision is much more than just sensitivity to light. The physiological process of seeing involves the registering of light impressions on the sensitive cells in the eye, both rods and cones, and the transmission of signals corresponding to these impressions, via the optic nerve, to the brain. These signals contain information about the colour, intensity and contrast of the visual stimuli which are then interpreted, principally by comparison with previously stored sensory impressions in the memory, to make a recognisable picture. Interpretation is affected by a variety of physiological and psychological factors as well as by the nature of the physical signal itself. Critical aspects of the interpretation process are dissemination of detail, colour recognition and the organisation of the elements of the picture so that it can be readily identified – all features of visual perception which the Gestalt psychologists of the 1920s and 1930s explained as the 'exactnesses' of the mind.

The vision process is therefore prone to various influences which can affect the perception of detail, brightness, contrast and colour. Through tests such as those used to examine for colour blindness, the Camouflage Section was able to identify optical illusion-type effects and other methods of visual confusion utilising particular mixes of colours, all of which were incorporated in systems of protective painting for ships.

Practical tests on all these camouflage schemes and effects were carried out using techniques similar to those employed by Norman Wilkinson's group of Admiralty camouflage technicians. Model ships were painted in accordance with both the existing 'schools' of camouflage and, as research developed, the new combinations of shapes and colours. These models were deployed on a miniature ocean under various conditions of light and atmosphere and evaluated, first by visual comparison and then by measurement with photometric devices against predetermined control values.

Trials were also conducted to assess the camouflage qualities of different colours. Utilising what were then relatively primitive visibility scale instruments, they were able to determine the range and conditions at which given hues and densities of colour appeared more or less visible. Thus, a scale of responses was compiled against which standardised paint pigments could be specified and manufactured.

The findings and recommendations of Loyd Jones' team were widely adopted in the anti-submarine tactics of the United States and other Allies. The importance of the Camouflage Section's work lay in its development of a wholly new understanding and scientific specification of the phenomena of visibility. To have achieved so much in such a short time – the Camouflage Section was closed in February 1919 – was itself a fitting tribute to the dedicated efforts of these scientists.

Whereas in the United Kingdom the Dazzle Section carried total responsibility for both the development and application of protective colouring designs, the situation was somewhat different in the United States. Another Camouflage Section under Henry Reuterdahl and quite separate from the Eastman Kodak Research Center was attached to the Emergency Fleet Corporation, an organisation which had been created to manage and operate vessels acquired by the Shipping Board specifically for the war effort. The painting of merchant vessels in camouflage colours was the exclusive concern of this Corporation. Furnished with the design and colouring recommendations from the Research Center, the Corporation's district camouflage advisors supervised the repainting of auxiliaries and other ships using their own dockyard pesonnel.

The Dazzle Section at Burlington House finally ceased operations on 31 January 1919. The Section's goals had been realised long before when, from early 1918, the fortunes of the war at sea had finally turned in the Allies' favour. At last it had been possible to strengthen the fighting units on the battlefields of Europe to the point where Germany was compelled to accept the terms of an armistice – President Woodrow Wilson's much-vaunted 'peace without victory'.

An interesting development some months before the war ended on 11 November 1918 was the transfer of the Dazzle Section from the Admiralty to the Controller General of Merchant Shipping. The Section continued to reside at the Royal Academy but this reorganisation hinted at the arrangements which were to prevail throughout World War II when separate camouflage units were set up for military and civilian applications.

The termination of hostilities provided the opportunity, as it did for so many other experimental practices, to assess just how effective camouflage methods had been. Much energy and time had been expended on developing techniques, the worth of which could now be either confirmed or refuted by evaluation of the numbers of ships they had saved. That losses generally had declined in the later stages of World War I was obvious but, as stated earlier, numerous other factors influenced this improvement.

While the war was still in progress the Admiralty had set up a Committee on Dazzle Painting whose task was to evaluate the benefits, if any, of the process. This committee compiled figures for almost 70,000 shipping movements between January and October 1918, just under half the total being of dazzled vessels, the remainder being of ships painted shades of neutral grey. Apart from the fact that these figures showed that ships generally were less likely to be attacked when sailing in convoy, regardless of their colouring, they suggested that dazzled ships were marginally more prone to attack than non-dazzled ships, in the approximate ratio 3:2, especially when in convoy formation. However, of the vessels that were attacked, the number of dazzled ships hit was marginally lower than the number of non-dazzled ships hit, the ratio being approximately 3:4, suggesting that the stark patterns of dazzle camouflage were able to confuse U-boat commanders and affect their aim.

The *De Kalb* was further repainted in 1918, in dazzle livery. She made eleven trooping voyages during her military career, commencing on 14 June 1917 as part of the convoy carrying the first troops of the American expeditionary force to France. In all, she transported 11,334 troops outward and, after the war's end, she repatriated 20,332 in eight homeward voyages. (*United States Naval Historical Center*)

An example of another camouflage trick from World War I: the *Antigone* (ex-*Neckar*), American troopship, with silhouette of false destroyer escort painted on her side. (*United States Naval Historical Center*)

These statistics, while not entirely discrediting dazzle painting, did not particularly favour it either. Of the ships assessed by the committee, most of those that were dazzled were bigger ships presenting a more conspicuous target, some 25 per cent of the total number measuring over 6,000 gross tons, while the non-dazzled ships were much smaller, less than 6 per cent of the total number being over 6,000 gross tons. This imbalance of size raised serious questions about the credibility of the committee's assessment. Nevertheless, the committee gave as its recommendations that dazzle painting in the future should be applied only to ships not sailing in convoy, or where their owners specifically requested it. It was claimed too by the Admiralty that U-boat commanders had been unaffected by the bizarre abstractions of dazzled camouflage but after the war ended it was discovered that special training on dazzled targets had been given to U-boat crews at Kiel where a Hamburg Amerika Line ship had been specially repainted.

Other opinions on dazzle painting also differed sharply with those of the Admiralty Committee and were, in the main, more supportive of the system. In a letter to Norman Wilkinson in December 1918, Lord Pirrie, the shipowner, confirmed the positive achievements of dazzle painting. In it he declared, 'I am sure the splendid work you have been doing has safeguarded hundreds of lives and ships, believe me'. If anyone was in a position to know, he was. Whatever its true impact, the popular view was that dazzle painting had indeed been very successful, a notion that was neatly summed up in the verse by G F Norton:

Captain Schmidt at the periscope,
You need not fall and faint,
For it's not the vision of drug and dope,
But only the dazzle-paint.
And you're done, you're done, my pretty Hun.
You're done in the big blue eye,
By painter-men with a sense of fun,
And their work has just gone by.
Cheero!
A convoy safely by!

The *Mount Vernon* (ex-*Kronprinzessin Cecilie*), seen postwar but still sporting deliberately contrasted funnel colours. Compare this with the picture on page 69. (*Frank Braynard*)

One particularly interesting conclusion drawn from the British experience of dazzle painting, irrefutably substantiated in the reports from merchant ship captains, revealed another benefit of the system. Irrespective of the merits or otherwise of camouflage as a protection for the vessels themselves, it was noted that the presence of dazzle colours on a ship had a profound and positive effect on the morale of her crew.

As befitted their more orderly and logical approach to the subject the Americans had also recorded figures on the effects of camouflage. In contrast to the British statistics, these showed that camouflage, and dazzle painting in particular, had been extremely effective. Over the 22 months of its existence, the Eastman Kodak Camouflage Section had prepared a total of 495 different painting designs of which 302 were applied to merchant vessels and the remainder to naval vessels. Approximately 1,250 vessels in total were camouflaged in one form or other from 1 March 1918 onwards. After that date some ninety-six ships of all types were lost, of which only eighteen were camouflaged. Of these eighteen, four were sunk in collision accidents and three were mined, so less than one per cent of the vessels that had been camouflaged were sunk by torpedo – indisputable proof of the value of protective colouring.

For the merchant auxiliaries that survived, World War I had ended none too soon. For some, national service continued for many months more with repatriation duties but at least they no longer had to contend with the insidious wartime hazards of torpedo and mine. When this work was completed the ships were 'demobbed' one by one and returned to their normal employment: sparkling company colours to hide drab grey or psychedelic dazzle; extravagance and luxury to replace austerity and discomfort; and cheerful travellers replacing the hundreds of impersonal brown uniforms.

World War II, Before and After

WORLD WAR I may have ended and the need for camouflage protection may have passed but dazzle painting continued to make the headlines in a controversy that at times exposed passions as intense as those that first led to its conception. Following the cessation of hostilities a number of claims were deposited with the Royal Commission for Awards to Inventors seeking an award for initiating the principle of dazzle painting, suggesting that Norman Wilkinson was not entitled to claim the credit for being its originator.

So many, indeed, were the rival claims that the Admiralty set up a Committee of Enquiry under Admiral Farquhar, which presided until October 1922, to consider the issue and decide who should be rewarded for, and acknowledged as, the inventor of the scheme. Such were the legal overtones of the proceedings that each claimant was represented by King's Council. Norman Wilkinson called Admiral Sir Lewis Bayley, Captain Henry Kendall of Canadian Pacific and Commodore Bertram Hayes of the White Star Line as witnesses in support of his case.

A Captain F M Livingston-James of the East Lancashire Regiment indicated that he had submitted his 'Notes on the Principles of Camouflage at Sea' to the Admiralty on the 2 March 1918 and had followed this up with a visit to the Dazzle Section, on 10 September 1918, to discuss his ideas with Norman Wilkinson. His claims rested on the assertion that the Dazzle Section had in fact adopted and implemented these ideas.

A more detailed submission was made by Professor John Graham Kerr (later Sir John Graham Kerr), Regius Professor of Zoology at the University of Glasgow. He informed the committee that he had first approached Winston Churchill, then the First Sea Lord, by letter as early as 24 September 1914 with his proposals on protective colouring for

The scheme that was endorsed by the Admiralty's Committee on Awards to Inventors – Norman Wilkinson's dazzle painting system shown here on the *Aquitania*, seen from the stern at Brest on 22 February 1919. (*Imperial War Museum*)

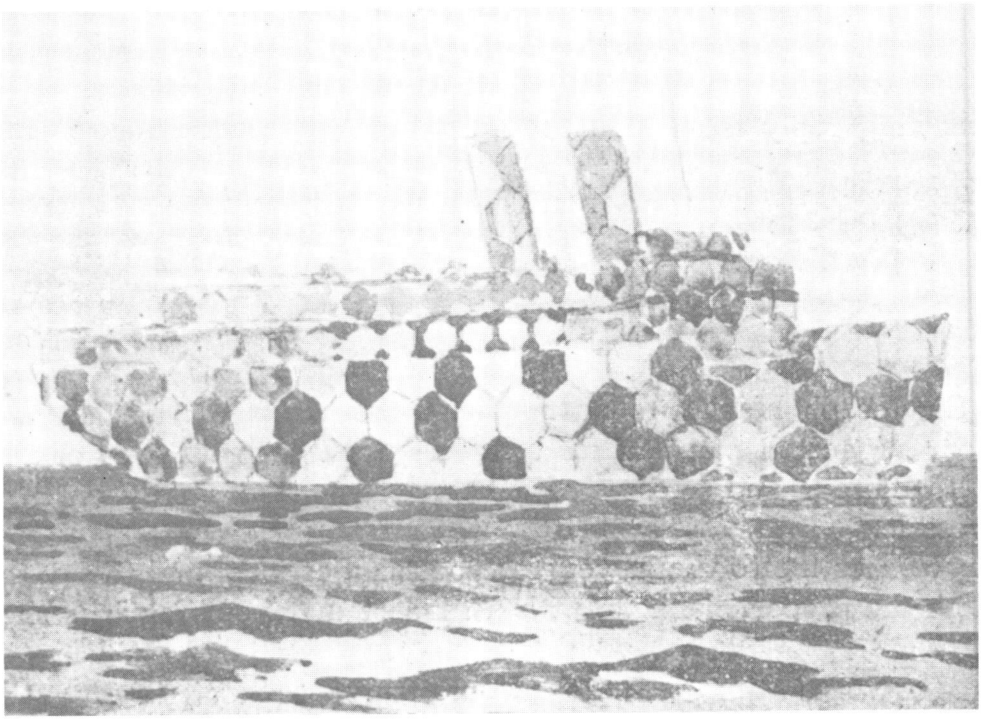

Artist's impression of one of Archibald Phillip's ambitious camouflage schemes based on a symmetrical, repeated pattern of hexagrams. (*Public Record Office*)

ships. He had enclosed a copy of his paper, entitled 'Professor Graham Kerr's Method of Diminishing the Visibility of Ships at a Distance', a document which explained his techniques for making vessels less visible by breaking up the continuity of surface and outline using compensative shading, or 'parti-colouring' as he called it. A further approach to the Admiralty had been made on 14 June 1915 but neither elicited a positive response.

Professor Kerr's schemes seemed to lean heavily on the Laws of Counter-Shading which had been formulated even earlier by the American painter, Abbott Henderson Thayer. Also, like the scheme of another claimant, the artist P Tudor Hart, who proposed the painting of ships in multi-coloured 3in squares in a form of 'pointilism' or in blocks of vertical and horizontal zig-zag lines, Professor Kerr's method sought to reduce ships' visibility. As the enquiry was concerned with dazzle painting, the committee was obliged anyway to disregard these claims on these grounds. Tudor Hart had in fact won support from the Admiralty in 1917 for experimentation with his systems at their expense. These tests were inconclusive and ultimately nothing came of them.

The instigators of two further submissions claimed that credit for the dazzle technique should rightfully belong to them. Mr J M Baker, who described himself as a 'life-long student of colour, shade and effect', informed the committee that he had conceived the idea after observing in detail ships anchored in the River Mersey in different states of light and weather; he had also first coined the term 'dazzle' in February 1915 when he had communicated his ideas to Mr Churchill. (In actual fact it is far more likely that the word dazzle was an extrapolation of Thayer's term 'razzle-dazzle' which he had used as early as 1909 as a description for certain forms of natural camouflage.)

A stronger challenge yet was made by a Mr Archibald Phillips, a Liverpool art dealer, who had sent a veritable catalogue of camouflage designs, some described as having a 'dazzle effect', to the Admiralty on 9 and 28 May 1915. One of these designs was based on a peculiar mosaic pattern system which produced a strongly three-dimensional stepped effect. Phillips went to considerable expense in the promotion of his claim, publishing an elaborate booklet entitled 'Suggestions for the Camouflage or Dazzle of British Merchant Ships in the Great War'.

It was all in vain, however, for Admiral Farquhar's committee found in favour of Norman Wilkinson who, anyway, had never suggested that the principles of his dazzle

The *Neuralia*, restored to peacetime trooping duties after serving as a hospital ship during World War I. (*World Ship Photo Library*)

Bibby Line's *Somersetshire* of 1921, one of the first new generation of Board of Trade peacetime troopships built between the wars. (*Tom Rayner*)

techniques were a unique conception. The committee stated that he was entitled to claim the credit for the purpose and the method of the dazzle scheme and that he was not indebted to any prior communications by others to the Admiralty. His reward was a single payment of £2,000. Though the other claims were dismissed, the Committee of Enquiry made it clear in their letters of rejection that they both recognised and respected that the efforts of each of the other scheme's promoters had been 'governed by a patriotic motive and spirit'.

The momentum of research into camouflage technology that had been initiated in 1917 and so abruptly ended in 1919 was not reactivated until 1935, and then only in the United States. During that year the United States Navy made funds available to the Naval Research Laboratory to permit the recommencement of studies and tests on low visibility camouflage at San Diego, California. Although the United States had adopted an isolationist stance in world affairs, and it was still some years before the Pearl Harbor attack was to draw the country into World War II, the research effort continued. In 1936 the scope of these studies was expanded; in 1939 they were intensified further.

During the 1930s a further group of modern troopships was built for the Board of Trade. Shown here are P&O's *Ettrick* and ... (*Tom Rayner*)

Prior to that camouflage had become a forgotten art, although the United States Navy did maintain its Camouflage Training School throughout the interwar period. The wartime auxiliaries had, with few exceptions, returned to commercial service by the early 1920s. In the United Kingdom peacetime trooping had been resumed by the chartered vessels of the Board of Trade fleet, wearing the now familiar livery of white hull with blue stripe and yellow funnels. The Mercantile Marine Department of the Board of Trade had taken over responsibility for trooping from the Ministry of Shipping at the end of the war.

In America a large number of the former German vessels appropriated for troop carrying to France from April 1917, when the United States entered the war, had been retained in the Reserve Fleet, only to be laid up in backwater creeks and rivers all round the Union. These vessels were mostly redesignated US Army transports and as such were repainted, with distinctive funnel colours and their USAT identities on both sides of their bows. They saw little activity thereafter and by the outbreak of World War II, when they could once more have made a valuable contribution to the allied effort, the vivid red streaks of rust proclaimed the extent of their deterioration and the majority went instead to the scrapyard. Only the *George Washington*, fondly remembered by the dough-boy armies as the 'Big George' and now renamed the USS *Catlin*, and the former *America*, as the USS *Edmund B Alexander*, saw troop carrying service for the second time in their careers.

... Bibby Line's *Devonshire*, seen post-World War II. (*Tom Rayner*)

Early in World War II, the *Ile de France* with grey hull and French Line red and black funnels. (*Cie Générale Maritime*)

By 1940 most auxiliaries had settled on standard navy grey for their protective colouring. Seen here are the *Empress of Canada* and ... (*Imperial War Museum*)

... Shaw Savill & Albion's *Dominion Monarch.* (*Author's collection*)

WHEN WAR BROKE OUT in Europe in September 1939, Britain was not as well prepared as the United States in respect of colouring techniques for the protection of merchant vessels carrying vital supplies. Experience from World War I led to the immediate reintroduction of convoy practices but whereas the principle threat in the earlier conflict had been U-boats, attack from the air now added a new dimension of danger. As the extent of this aerial threat to shipping came to be appreciated, so camouflage measures were developed to provide a degree of protection against this too.

World War II also witnessed the rapid development of radar, a prewar invention, which permitted ships to be located even when they were invisible to the naked eye. The role of camouflage in these circumstances had to be reappraised. Reverting to some extent to the camouflage principles of late World War I, designs were revamped which would make it difficult to ascertain the identity of a ship or its true bearing once it had been spotted.

At the beginning of the war there was considerable uncertainty as to what were the approved concealment schemes or even what government department was responsible for advising on these matters. In fact, both the Admiralty and the Ministry of Shipping, which had been reformed in 1939, made recommendations for the repainting of merchant vessels engaged in war service in two-tone or three-tone grey, each colour based on different reflection factors, but the information was so badly publicised that numerous freelance schemes characterised the early months of the war. Commonplace combinations were darkened hull and superstructure with normal, peacetime funnel colours, or an ochre shade for the upperworks with black funnels similar to the colours painted on many P&O ships of the interwar era. The *Aquitania* is reported to have been repainted with navy blue hull and grey/blue superstructure during this period but, in the absence of colour photographs, it is impossible to corroborate this description.

Gradually, all ships conformed to the neutral grey shades that had been typical of early World War I. In spite of the not inconsiderable success of dazzle painting, no attempt was made to reintroduce it, at least not in its original form and not on the majority of British mercantile auxiliaries. From April 1941, aware of the threat of aerial attack, Admiralty recommendations for merchant ship colouring called for the use of MSS (Merchant Ship Sides) mid-grey and MSD (Merchant Ship Decks) dark grey.

While Britain was engaged in establishing camouflage colour conventions for her merchant fleet, Germany was preoccupied with getting as many of her dispersed passenger ships home as possible. Painted disguise was a frequently used method of deception in the various attempts to make it back to the Fatherland.

Left: Norddeutscher Lloyd's flagship, the *Bremen*, arriving at Bremerhaven from Polarnöye on 13 December 1939. Her upperworks have been darkened. (*L L von Münching*)

Above right: Sailors paint the *Columbus*'s deck fittings as part of the process of darkening her prior to her abortive dash to Germany. (*Capt Otto Giese – collection of C S Ashdown*)

The *Bremen*, flagship of the German merchant marine, was in New York just before war was declared. On 30 August 1939 she sailed without passengers, and under a veil of secrecy, bound for Murmansk, the German-Soviet non-aggression pact guaranteeing a friendly reception for her at this Arctic port. In early December 1939 she made her way discreetly down the Norwegian coast, being needed for conversion to a troopship in readiness for Operation Sealion, the impending invasion of the British Isles. When she arrived at Bremerhaven it was quite evident that she had been darkened while at sea to diminish the brightness of her normally white superstructure. Apparently, en route she had also flown the Soviet flag for a period, but it is highly unlikely that this would have fooled the Royal Navy.

Meanwhile, her fleetmate *Columbus* was making her ill-fated bid to make it home from Vera Cruz, Mexico, where she had sought sanctuary after her Caribbean pleasure cruise was interrupted by the outbreak of hostilities. Prior to sailing for home, the *Columbus*' master had his ship darkened in like fashion to the *Bremen* but, in addition, the tops of her funnels were painted black. In the event none of this particularly aided the ship. On her voyage north she hugged the American coast for as long as she could, tailed by a succession of American warships, but, on 19 December, immediately upon leaving the safety of neutral American waters, she was intercepted by the destroyer HMS *Hyperion* and was scuttled by her crew.

If the disguise adopted by the *Columbus* was hopeful, then that applied to the Deutsche Ost Afrika Line vessel *Windhuk* was extremely ambitious. Her twin funnels were painted black with white rings and she sailed into the Brazilian port of Santos on 7 December 1939 bearing the name *Santos Maru*. Only a passing glance at the Osaka Shosen Kaisha vessel she was mimicking was needed to show that the *Windhuk* bore no resemblance to her whatever. The *Windhuk* was a cruiser-sterned ship whereas the *Santos Maru* was counter-sterned and had only a single funnel. When Brazil entered the war, the *Windhuk* was seized. Declared a war prize, she was sold to the Americans on 12 May 1942. Under their control her funnels were reduced to just one during reconstruction into the troop transport USS *Lejeune*.

The outbreak of war also saw the re-emergence of neutrality markings on the vessels of non-belligerent countries. Initially, these were displayed by the vessels of, among

The repainting complete, the *Columbus* is anchored off Vera Cruz ready to sail.
(*Capt Otto Giese – collection of C S Ashdown*)

Intercepted by HMS *Hyperion* on 19 December 1939, the *Columbus*'s crew scuttled their ship. As special squads opened her sea cocks and lit fires aboard her, the remainder of her complement took to the boats. The black tops added to her normal funnel colours are clearly seen in this picture.
(*Capt Otto Giese – collection of C S Ashdown*)

The Deutsche Ost Afrika Line's *Windhuk* arriving at Santos, Brazil, very thinly disguised as the *Santos Maru*.
(*Arnold Kludas*)

The real *Santos Maru* of Osaka Shosen Kaisha. She looked nothing like the disguised *Windhuk*, as this photograph demonstrates. (*World Ship Photo Library*)

Neutrality markings were widely adopted early in World War II and there were numerous variations on the theme: the *Nieuw Amsterdam* and ... (*Tom Rayner*)

... the *Statendam* display only their names and country of ownership. The just-launched destroyer in the foreground of this picture, taken on 12 October 1939, is the *Tjerk Hiddes*. (L L von Münching)

By May 1940 when this photograph was taken of the port of Rotterdam under bombardment, Dutch vessels had had their national flag added to their sides. The *Veendam* is on the right, the *Boschdijk* is astern of her and at the extreme left is the *Statendam*, ablaze from stem to stern. (*P Mulder*)

Norwegian America Line's *Stavangerfjord* displaying only her name and national flag. (*Tom Rayner*)

The *Serpa Pinto* of Cia Colonial de Navegacao. Her national flag separates her name from her country of origin. National colours were also painted on hatch covers in World War II, to aid identification from the air. (*Tom Rayner*)

others, Spain, Sweden, Brazil, Italy, the United States, Japan, Greece and The Netherlands. As events developed, the neutrality of the last two countries was flagrantly violated, while America and Brazil on the one hand and Italy and Japan on the other, joined the Allies and Axis forces respectively. Ironically, following the fall of France the ships of the Vichy regime, which declared itself to be neutral, were once more repainted in their civilian colours with full neutrality identifying marks.

The traditional auxiliary roles of hospital ship, troopship and AMC were also revived from the beginning of World War II but on a scale that was truly vast compared with World War I. Germany commissioned many of her passenger liners as hospital ships, stationing them in the Baltic where they were needed to treat casualties from the fighting in Poland and, later, Russia. Britain, Japan and America also commissioned large numbers of vessels of this type. As in World War I there were variations to the stipulated hospital ship colouring arrangements, with significant differences to the width of the hull band while, on one or two ships, the Red Cross emblem on the funnel was encircled. These inconsistencies caused confusion with a completely different type of vessel which figured prominently in World War II – the diplomat refugee or repatriation vessel. Several colouring alternatives were also applied to these ships but one pair, the Italian sisters *Duilio* and *Giulio Cesare*, were painted in what, at first glance, looked like routine hospital ship colours. Engaged for a series of repatriation voyages from East Africa around the Cape to Italy in the Spring of 1942, the only means by which their distinctive

Cie Maritime Belge's *Baudoinville* seen at Antwerp early in 1940. (*Tom Rayner*)

Another Dutch vessel in neutrality markings, Royal Interocean Line's *Tegelberg* at Cape Town.
(*Tom Rayner*)

Neutral American vessels also showed differences in their neutrality markings: the *Siboney*, now owned by American Export Lines, has her company name and national flag on her sides.
(*Tom Rayner*)

The *Panama* of the Panama Railroad Company displays only a single national flag ...
(*Tom Rayner*)

role could be determined visually was their lack of a hull band and the colouring of their funnels which displayed the Swiss Cross, not the Red Cross.

The *Duilio* and *Giulio Cesare* both became victims of the war. They were first scuttled at Trieste in September 1943, at the time of the collapse of Italy. Later, they were raised by the Germans but before they could be thoroughly restored and put to useful employment they were sunk in air attacks on Trieste, the *Duilio* on 6 July 1944 and the *Giulio Cesare* on 25 August 1944. When the Allies entered the port on 3 May 1945 the sister ships were found capsized and fit only for scrap.

... while the United States Lines' newly completed flagship *America* is identified by her own name, her owner's name and the flag of the United States. (*Tom Rayner*)

Italian and Japanese merchant ships which were able to claim neutrality until June 1940 and December 1941 respectively, showed their status with their national flag alone: the *Hokoku Maru*. (*Mitsui-OSK Lines*)

The *Brazil Maru*. Her sinking in a torpedo attack on 5 August 1942 ranks as one of the worst Japanese losses of World War II. (*Mitsui-OSK Lines*)

No battledress, of any variety, was of value in protecting ships from magnetic mines for they distinguished neither friend nor foe. Hiding behind camouflage or displaying hospital ship or neutrality colours made no difference. The Union Castle liner *Dunbar Castle*, sunk in the Dover Strait on 9 January 1940. (*British & Commonwealth Shipping Company*)

Consort to the *Rex*, the *Conte di Savoia* is shown laid up after Italy had declared war, her neutrality marking amidships almost completely faded away. The *Rex* too had her national flag painted on her sides from September 1939 to June 1940. (*Aldo Fraccaroli*)

Italia Line's flagship *Rex*. A peacetime view before neutrality markings were painted on her hull. (*L L von Münching*)

From June 1940, after the fall of France, ships of the Vichy regime claimed neutrality and were painted accordingly. Shown here is Cie de Navigation Paquet's *Chella*. (*L L von Münching*)

The *Tabora* of the Deutsche Ost Afrika in a hospital ship colour scheme that hardly accords with the regulations of the Geneva Convention. (*Tom Rayner*)

French Line's *Champlain* sunk off La Pallice, near Bordeaux, in June 1940 – a poor but rare German wartime photograph with an E-boat in the left foreground. (*L L von Münching*)

Holland America Line's *Spaarndam* in the mouth of the River Thames, November 1939. (*L L von Münching*)

Many more ships were taken over as hospital ships during World War II than in World War I: the German hospital ship *Wilhelm Gustloff*, former Kraft durch Freude cruise liner, had the Red Crosses on her funnel enclosed in circles. (*Arnold Kludas*)

The German *Stuttgart* was another former KdF cruise ship. (*Arnold Kludas*)

Norddeutscher Lloyd's *Berlin*, built in 1925. (*Arnold Kludas*)

The *Tairea* of British India Line, British hospital ship number 35, at Port Tewfik, Suez, and ... (*Imperial War Museum*)

... her sister ship *Talamba*, hospital ship number 43. (*Tom Rayner*)

The Dutch naval hospital ship *Tjitjalengka*, number D3. (*Imperial War Museum*)

Sister ship to the ill-fated *Athenia*, the *Letitia* served as the Canadian hospital ship number 66. (*Real Photos*)

The *El Nil*, hospital ship number 53. Note how the Red Cross on her funnel is not painted but is a fixture carrying lights for night time illumination. (*W Haig Perry*)

The Italian liner *Saturnia* was seized by the Americans during World War II and pressed into service as the hospital ship *Frances Y Slanger*, named after the first American nurse to lose her life in the conflict. (*Antonio Scrimali*)

The American hospital ship *Comfort*, rebuilt from the Ward Line Steamship *Yucatan* (ex *Havana*). (*World Ship Photo Library*).

Japan also commissioned a number of hospital ships: the *Takasago Maru*. Note her number in Japanese characters. (*Mitsui-OSK Lines*)

The *Hikawa Maru*, the former hospital ship, seen at Yokohama. She was the only major, deep sea Japanese passenger liner to survive the war. (*Yoshitatsu Fukawa*)

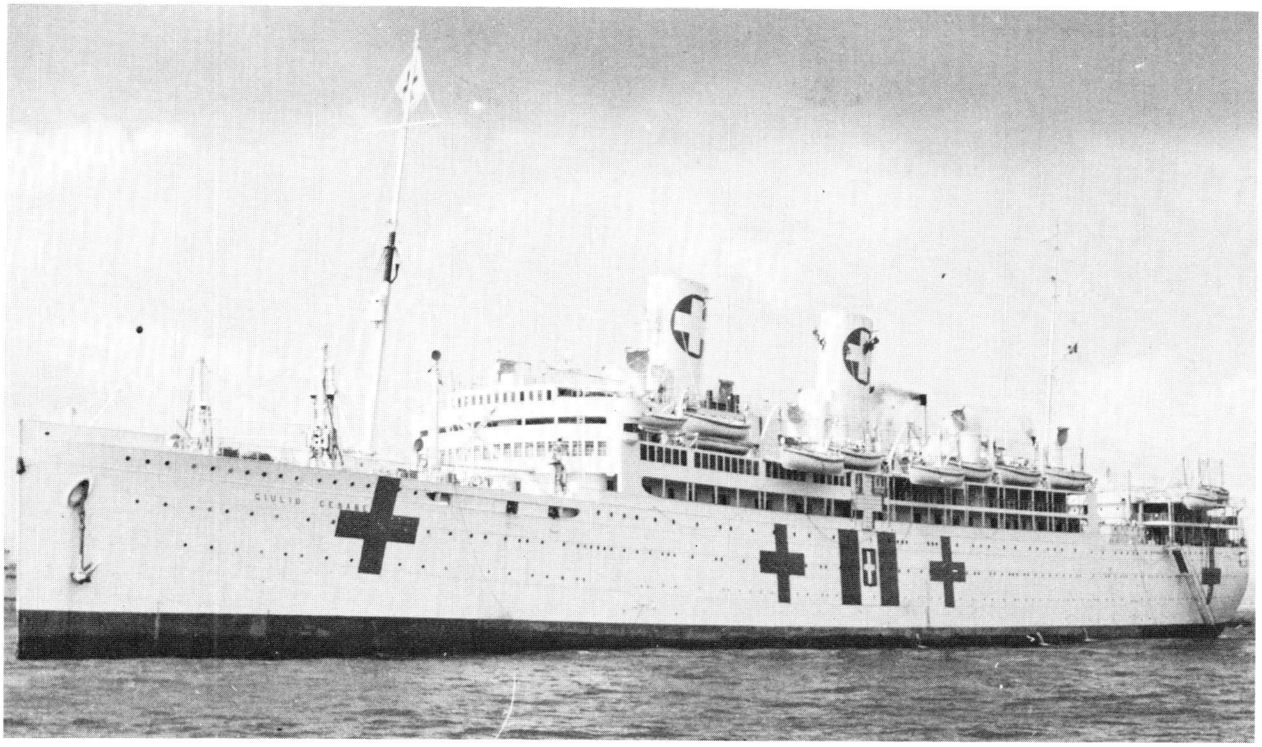

PERHAPS THE TWO MOST famous diplomat ships of World War II were the Swedish Amerika Line fleetmates *Gripsholm* and *Drottningholm* which made a number of voyages under charter to the International Red Cross repatriating exchanged prisoners of war, invalids and other displaced persons. For this work they adopted a unique colour scheme which was a development of the neutrality markings they had been obliged to adopt at the commencement of the war. To these markings was added the word PROTECTED in conspicuous lettering. Later it was replaced with the legend DIPLOMAT, displayed equally prominently.

Another vessel taken up for a mercy voyage under the sanction of the International Red Cross was the Nippon Yusen Kaisha liner *Awa Maru*, but her diplomat duties ended in a less auspicious fashion. To quote the Lloyd's War Loss Records, she was 'sunk whilst

Easily mistaken for a hospital ship, the Italian steamer *Giulio Cesare* was actually employed as a diplomat repatriation vessel. Her distinctive role is signified by the absence of a hull band, the Swiss Crosses on her funnels (reversed white on red) and the Italian flag painted on her side. The *Giulio Cesare* is seen at Gibraltar in 1942 prior to evacuating, with her sister ship *Duilio*, 11,000 Italian civilians from Abyssinia to Italy via the Cape of Good Hope. (*Imperial War Museum*)

The *Giulio Cesare* and *Duilio* were sunk in Italian coastal waters in the later stages of the war. The wrecked *Duilio* is seen at Vallone di Zaule, near Trieste. (*L L von Münching*)

The most famous pair of World War II diplomat ships were the Swedish America Line pair *Gripsholm* and …
(*Author's collection*)

… *Drottningholm*. In this view, taken in 1943, the *Drottningholm* displays the word PROTECTED on the side of her hull. She was repatriating wounded British prisoners from German prisoner of war camps across the North Sea in consort with the British hospital ship *Atlantis*.
(*Imperial War Museum*)

Later, the *Drottningholm* carried the word DIPLOMAT on her side in similar fashion to the *Gripsholm*.
(*World Ship Photo Library*)

The unfortunate *Awa Maru*, sunk during a diplomat voyage on 1 April 1945. She is seen here in navy grey but at the time of her loss she was painted overall sea green with white crosses on the sides of her hull. (*Nippon Yusen Kaisha*)

sailing under Allied safe conduct'. The date was 1 April 1945. The *Awa Maru* was returning to Tsuruga, on the west coast of Honshu, from a voyage to Hong Kong, Saigon, Singapore, Djakarta and other ports to carry supplies for Allied prisoners of war and other civilian internees in Japanese custody. The submarine responsible for the sinking was the USS *Queenfish* whose master explained, in defence of his actions, that in the murky, overcast conditions the liner had been mistaken for a warship. For once the concealment value of ship colouring had backfired for, unlike the other diplomat vessels, the *Awa Maru* was not painted in true Red Cross or neutrality identifying colours but in an overall coat of green paint of the same type widely used for Japanese warships. The only indication of her protected status were white crosses painted on her sides and the flag of the International Red Cross flying at her mast head. The failure to identify the *Awa Maru* proved to be a costly mistake, resulting in the loss of over 2,000 lives, including that of a newborn infant delivered while the ship was at sea.

It is only natural to wonder, of course, whether this incident happened because of doubts concerning Japan's integrity in respect of her use of protected status; there may have been the suspicion that the *Awa Maru* was in reality being used to convey armaments, troops and other war materials. This is pure speculation, but there were good grounds for such misgivings. The Japanese had already demonstrated that they were prepared to exploit the status of immunity enjoyed by hospital ships. Indeed, under their code of military ethics, hospital ship livery was one of the most effective forms of disguise, providing the ideal, innocent front for otherwise hostile activities. An example of this was the hospital ship *Tatibana Maru* which was intercepted in the Banda Sea on 6 August 1945 by American destroyers. Escorted into port and then inspected, she was found to be carrying machine guns, packed ammunition marked 'Medical Supplies' and a quantity of other armaments. Bandages were removed from her 1,500 'patients' to reveal that the majority had no wounds whatever.

It is worth mentioning here that, prior to World War II, the Germans too had resorted

Ships of the Kraft durch Freude sail to Vigo, Spain on 16 May 1939, led by the pocket battleship *Admiral Graf Spee*, to embark the Luftwaffe Condor Legion. From left to right the *Robert Ley, Wilhelm Gustloff* and *Der Deutsche.* (*Heinz Schön*)

to this 'Trojan horse' approach to deception when, to avoid undue and unwelcome publicity, they adopted the same strategy to ship the notorious Condor Legion to Spain for the duration of the Spanish Civil War. Conveniently, the government-owned cruise fleet of the *Kraft durch Freude* movement was at their disposal for the task and these vessels were mustered for one of the most bizarre military transportation exercises ever. It was so discreet that there were few outward signs as to its true purpose. The service personnel were deliberately dressed in the civilian attire of typical cruise holidaymakers and encouraged to line the rails and indulge in deck recreations, apparently enjoying a jolly, carefree time. When, in May 1939, the same ships were used to return the battle-hardened fighter squadrons to Germany, following the much publicised outrage of Guernica, it was without any pretence at modesty. The ships sailed in convoy formation, led by the pocket battleship *Admiral Graf Spee*, their purpose widely advertised. When they arrived at Hamburg, they were greeted with a military style reception, many leading figures from the Nazi hierarchy being present on the quayside.

From June 1940, Germany commenced preparations for the invasion of Britain, for which an immense fleet of support and supply ships was assembled in the ports along the Channel and North Sea coastlines. The express passenger liners *Bremen* and *Europa* were among the vessels taken over for Operation Sealion. They were earmarked for a special troop movement exercise which involved delivering upwards of 10,000 crack

The *Bremen* painted in dazzle colours in readiness for Operation Sealion, the invasion of Britain. (*L L von Münching*)

Many allied troopships continued to be painted in neutral grey for the duration of the war: the *Nieuw Amsterdam*'s generally grey hull is worn and patchy in this view in port, with a Canadian serviceman looking on. (*L L von Münching*)

troops each per voyage from a base in Norway to the northeast coast of Scotland and England. The intention was to create a pincer movement which would tie up Britain's defences on two fronts. Both vessels were given striking camouflage colours and had huge apertures cut in their sides to expedite the embarkation and disembarkation of the troops. When the Luftwaffe failed to subdue the Royal Air Force in the Battle of Britain, Operation Sealion was postponed then cancelled and the twin giants were consequently laid up at Bremerhaven.

The conquest of much of Europe guaranteed for Germany, for the time being at least, plentiful supplies of raw materials, food and industrial capacity permitting the momentum of *blitzkrieg* to be maintained. In Britain, the situation was rather different. The economic strain of the war already necessitated dependence on the United States for armaments and other vital supplies. The Neutrality Act embargoed the direct supply of arms to Britain by America, but help was nevertheless forthcoming, at a price, through a series of

In this photograph, taken of the *Nieuw Amsterdam*, the grey paint on her hull is of a darker tone. She bears a strong resemblance to the *Queen Elizabeth* ... (*World Ship Photo Library*)

... also seen here in an aerial photograph. The *Queen Elizabeth* commenced her career in auxiliary colours and it was six years before she was to don her Cunard livery for the first time. (*World Ship Photo Library*)

The painting of troopships at different periods in either overall light grey or overall dark grey was quite common. This is clearly revealed in these shots of the *Pasteur*. Here she is dark grey ... (*Imperial War Museum*)

novel deals worked out by President Franklin D Roosevelt and Prime Minister Winston Churchill. First, the 'cash and carry' policy provided for the indirect supply, through Canada, of essential weapons, vehicles and ammunition. Later, the 'lend lease' scheme permitted the direct transhipment of war materials from United States ports. All these movements tied up a huge fleet of ships whose ability to get their valuable cargoes safely across the Atlantic was of paramount importance. From the summer of 1940, Britain had stood alone in the front line of freedom, a solitary position she continued to hold for the next year and a half. At all levels, both military and civilian, the British people made tremendous sacrifices. It is no exaggeration to say that the lifeline of supplies coming across the Atlantic meant the difference between continued opposition to the Nazi regime or financial collapse and capitulation. Winston Churchill himself said of this epic struggle on the Western Ocean, 'The Battle of the Atlantic was the dominating factor all through the war. Never for one moment could we forget that everything elsewhere depended on its outcome'.

... and here light grey. (*United States Coast Guard*)

The Armed Merchant Cruiser *Rawalpindi* prior to her encounter with the German battlecruisers *Scharnhorst* and *Gneisenau*. (*Imperial War Museum*)

To protect these supply ships from attack by U-boats and raiders, many passenger liners were again commissioned as auxiliary cruisers and some truly heroic deeds were performed by these frail, part-time warships. Perhaps more than any other incidents during those dark years of 1939 and 1940, the valiant self-sacrifice of the liners *Rawalpindi* and *Jervis Bay* summed up the defiant, unquenchable spirit of the people of these islands. Against all odds, they took on the full might of the German Navy knowing only too well that only one outcome was possible.

On 23 November 1939, the *Rawalpindi* was patrolling between Iceland and the Faeroes when she encountered the battlecruisers *Scharnhorst* and *Gneisenau* returning from a commerce raiding sortie in the Atlantic. Hopelessly outgunned and outmatched for speed, the *Rawalpindi* was quickly sunk, but not before she had been able to hit the *Gneisenau* with a salvo from her four starboard side 6in guns. Only thirty-seven of her 312-strong crew survived the confrontation. Among those lost was the *Rawalpindi*'s master, Captain Edward C Kennedy, father of the TV personality Ludovic Kennedy.

A year later, on 5 November 1940, when the *Jervis Bay* was sunk while defending convoy HX 84, her courageous action permitted the convoy to disperse and ensured that losses were minimal. The convoy was a thousand miles east of Newfoundland when it was attacked by the pocket battleship *Admiral Scheer*. Apart from the AMC *Jervis Bay*,

Listing and on fire, the auxiliary cruiser *Rawalpindi* is seen under attack from a German capital ship in this painting by Norman Wilkinson. Her attacker, on the horizon to the right, is mistakenly portrayed as the pocket battleship *Deutschland*, as it was believed originally that this ship had been responsible for sinking the *Rawalpindi*. (*P&O*)

the convoy was totally undefended but in order to provide the thirty-eight ships with the opportunity to scatter, she turned towards the enemy, steaming directly at the warship to engage. The hopelessly one-sided battle that ensued lasted for only one hour, the *Jervis Bay* taking the full brunt of the *Scheer*'s 11in guns while her own 6in pieces were largely ineffective. Nevertheless, the objective was achieved and by the time the *Jervis Bay* went down, some two hours later, night had fallen and the convoy ships had made good their escape concealed in the murk and behind smoke screens. Only six other vessels from HX 84 were sunk. The thirty-two remaining ships owed their survival to the 190 officers and men of the *Jervis Bay* who went down with their ship.

Neither the *Rawalpindi* nor the *Jervis Bay* were protected with anything more than a coat of neutral grey paint and no other, more sophisticated, method of concealment could have given either ship any greater protection in such circumstances. Nevertheless, the Admiralty's reversion to the camouflage standards of early World War I, for both auxiliaries and cargo ships, is interesting, suggesting as it does that contemporary thinking saw no particular advantage, in this new conflict, in the dazzled or splinter designs that Norman Wilkinson had pioneered. (It is interesting to note here that Norman Wilkinson did become involved in camouflage practices in World War II but he was concerned exclusively with airfield disguise.) Ironically, early in World War I, the Admiralty had at first regarded grey schemes as decidely disadvantageous for merchant ships, leading to confusion with warships and inviting attack. Clearly, by the time surface warships had identified and engaged a merchant auxiliary, arguments over the merits of opposing schemes were purely academic. However, other combatants in World War II continued to employ confusion schemes, demonstrating continuing faith in the value of this approach. British vessels were distinctive for their more or less uniform application of neutral grey, although, later in the war, many warships and some converted liners

Steaming towards her adversary, on the horizon to the right, and already surrounded by near misses, the *Jervis Bay*'s courageous sacrifice in protecting her convoy from the *Admiral Scheer* is depicted in this painting of the incident. (*Furness Withy*)

The Cunard liner *Aurania* with light grey superstructure and dark grey hull – the Admiralty Alternative Scheme. (*Imperial War Museum*)

P&O's *Cathay* seen on 19 July 1942 with, unusually, only one and a half funnels. (*United States Coast Guard*)

While research into alternative camouflage systems and techniques progressed, overall navy grey continued to be the protective order of the day – the best compromise measure for all average conditions: P&O Lines' *Corfu*. (*World Ship Photo Library*)

The *Queen of Bermuda* with her funnels reduced from three to two. (*United States Coast Guard*)

reverted to typical camouflage paint systems when, during the period 1942 to 1944, the Admiralty reverted to disruptive measures. This was very much as part of an allied policy which recognised that the advent of radar had made the pursuit of visual invisibility somewhat irrelevant. It was necessary instead, in certain sea areas where the use of electronic means of target identity was considered more widespread, to concentrate on confusing the enemy as to a ship's identity, speed and direction.

Despite the apparent lack of interest or conviction in more ambitious camouflage objectives, a great deal of research into marine camouflage techniques was carried out in Britain during the war. Work was carried out by the Admiralty Research Laboratory at

Cunard Line's *Queen Elizabeth*, bunkering. (A Duncan)

Teddington, Middlesex, in respect of naval applications and at the Directorate of Camouflage at Leamington Spa, Warwickshire, part of the Ministry of Home Security's Department of Research and Experiment. The Ministry of Home Security was itself a branch of the Home Office. Although the latter organisation was primarily concerned with concealment problems involving civilian vehicles and installations, collaboration between the two establishments was close and a Naval Section at the Leamington Spa centre was responsible for developing a range of techniques which were especially valuable to the war at sea. Another Admiralty section involved on the fringes of camouflage research was the Directorate of Miscellaneous Weapons Development.

In the main, coordination between Teddington and Leamington Spa involved the Admiralty section determining how ships should be painted, and the colours to be used, after which the Home Office developed a suitable design. All this information was then transferred to the ships concerned for implementation.

Of particular note among the techniques devised by the Directorate of Camouflage was a method of quantitative assessment of painted camouflage for ships. The assessment

Canadian Pacific's *Empress of Scotland* (ex-*Empress of Japan*), renamed after Japan joined the other Axis powers in December 1941. She is seen in Grand Harbour, Valletta. (*World Ship Photo Library*)

was based on the evaluation of each test scheme under the following conditions:

two viewing positions – from the surface and from the sky
three ranges – long, intermediate and close
five lighting conditions – overcast, thin overcast, weak sunlight, broken cloud and cloudless sky

The method employed a haze disc which was first set to invisibility and then to the position of first visibility of the target scheme. The two readings obtained were then compared, a process which was repeated for each of the conditions listed above. To further validate the quality of the data gathered, the relative brightness of the sky to the sea was established in all instances by taking photographs under a controlled procedure. Measurement of the resulting negatives was performed by the Physics Department of the Kodak Limited Research Laboratory at Wealdstone, Harrow, Middlesex. Though somewhat long-winded, this method of quantitative assessment was extremely dependable and provided much useful information on the suitability of alternative camouflage paint schemes.

The Leamington Spa camouflage establishment also carried out an analysis of the level of Purkinje Effect in sample pigments of Cobalt Blue and Ultramarine Blue which were proposed for use in marine concealment applications. The Purkinje Effect, named after the Czech physiologist Jan Evangelista Purkinje who discovered it, is a chameleon-like phenomenon in which red objects are preceived to fade faster than equally bright blue objects as the light intensity decreases. In fact the effect is not an illusion but the result of two little-known properties of the process of seeing – the ratio between photopic vision and scotopic vision. Photopic vision is how persons with normal sight see things in bright daylight with clear perception of detail and accurate recognition of colour. Scotopic vision, on the other hand, is how persons with normal sight see things in twilight with some perception of form but poor recognition of colour. The Purkinje Effect is greatly accentuated when blue and red pigments are used adjacently.

This research played a significant part in an attempt to create a true chameleon-like camouflage which would alter its colours in different lighting conditions to provide a measure of protection whatever the background against which a ship was viewed. Such an objective was clearly very ambitious but some success in this direction was achieved in

Dead in the water, the *Empress of Britain* on fire and listing after being attacked by enemy aircraft on 26 October 1940. Two days later she was finished off by torpedoes from a German U-boat. (*Imperial War Museum*)

The *Aquitania* again, looking imposing in her austere war garb. (*Real Photos*)

the development of what were known as refractive/reflective coatings, a sort of optical veneer which was capable of disrupting the path of light rays incident to and reflecting off the painted surface. The effect produced varied to some extent as the illumination altered from bright sunlight to dull overcast conditions. Unfortunately, however, these coatings were still of little benefit in reducing the hard shadows that formed on and around deck structures and which, infrequently, resulted in a vessel appearing as a near-silhouette against the sea.

During World War II, mere obfuscation from a potential surface assailant at extreme range was insufficient. The existence for the first time of powerful, long-range aircraft such as the Focke Wulf Fw 200c Condor, nicknamed the Scourge of the Atlantic, now meant that, once spotted, the target could rapidly be approached by the attacker, permitting a positive identification to be made. The problem of concealment at night was also a major issue, for ships were particularly visible in moonlight and the records showed that most submarine attacks occurred after twilight.

The Home Office camouflage establishment at Leamington Spa continued its work right through the war and beyond until, in May 1946, it was incorporated into the Inter-Services Camouflage Establishment at Erlestoke, near Devizes. Later still, it was renamed as the Admiralty Camouflage Research Station as an extension of the Admiralty Research Laboratory.

Through its involvement in the camouflage research trials described above, the Kodak Company in Britain had followed the lead set by its American parent concern during World War I. It was not, however, the only commercial organisation to be involved in this work during World War II. A considerably more active role was played by the General Electric Company. Much of the research effort of the GEC Research Laboratories (now the Hirst Research Centre) at Wembley, Middlesex, was devoted to determining techniques for resolving wartime visibility problems. Led by C C Paterson, Director of the Laboratories, the GEC team had some notable successes, particularly in the field of artificial lighting and in the laboratory synthesis of study environments for the purposes of analytical trials.

Especially useful was their compilation of a standard glossary of camouflage terms. This standardisation of camouflage language, which was adopted by all the Allies, greatly assisted the unambiguous exchange of information on the subject, particularly in the reports on full-scale field trials.

A major achievement by General Electric in the area of model test evaluation, which was of great importance for maritime camouflage, was the creation of a sophisticated Naval Camouflage Viewing Range. Since the early efforts of Norman Wilkinson and Loyd

Jones, little work had been done to improve the simulation of observing camouflaged ships at sea, a matter of prime significance if the results of model tests were to have any credibility. As the range of conditions in which ships might be viewed, as well as the viewing distances and working scales of models, was infinitely variable, so the requirements of a truly dependable all-purpose viewing range became more complex.

The viewing range constructed by General Electric to meet this demanding specification (described in Appendix 4) was developed around an approach to laboratory simulation called the analysis-synthesis method. This involved the precise determination, prior to experimentation, of what was to be viewed, in what conditions and for what purpose. Based on this analysis, the scene was then synthesised in model form concentrating on achieving the most accurate interpretation of all components (atmosphere, light, ship shape and texture etc) in order to provide the best simulation possible.

In the synthesis of the scene, considerable effort was made to achieve realistic and accurate representation and extreme care was taken over the construction of the object, the simulation of the illumination and atmosphere, and the projection of the background. The solid models were not only correctly painted but were carefully textured relative to their full-scale equivalent. Correct illumination, at the right intensity, was achieved for most applications by a mixture of directional and diffuse lighting but a great deal of trouble also had to be taken to ensure that it was the right colour temperature (*see glossary*). Atmospheric effects were found to be particularly difficult to calculate and recreate.

Visibility is influenced principally by two effects: the weakening of light as it passes through the atmosphere causing transmission losses and reduction of clarity, and a veil of illuminated haze or flare which exists to a greater or lesser extent over and around a scene. After much experimentation, a solution to the simulation of these atmospheric effects was found by the insertion of a haze box in the observer's plane of vision. This consisted of an inclined sheet of clear glass reflecting an illuminated opal which could have its intensity precisely adjusted either electronically or with graduated filters.

The most essential requirement in the viewing arrangement was to maintain, as correctly as possible, the natural perspective of the parts of the scene as presented to the observer. Nevertheless, to simulate realistic viewing conditions, observations were made on the range with 7 × 50 night glasses as well as by the naked eye, even though binoculars introduced stereoscopic and convergence effects to the image. These problems were to some extent alleviated by the use of suitable collimating lenses. In fact, viewing of the models was indirect because the observer actually saw a virtual image produced by a negative lens.

As it was intended that the viewing range should be used to evaluate camouflaged ships seen either against the sky on the horizon, against the sea, or hull down to varying extents, it was also necessary to light the models accurately to known conditions of sunlight with the sun at the correct elevation relative to the height and range of the observer. All these factors were addressed and answered satisfactorily.

Assessment of camouflage samples was by the describable criteria method, in which degrees of visibility, like those which would be encountered at sea, were predetermined for purposes of comparison. No attempt was made to use any numerical scale of visibility. Instead, physical constraints on the range were varied to produce the individual criteria or degrees of visibility determined. For each task three visibility criteria were established and for a typical camouflage evaluation exercise they might have been:

1 'Cannot see anything'
2 'Can just see a ship, but cannot identify it'
3 'Can see the ship clearly and can identify it'

The observer's task was to adhere strictly to these criteria throughout a series of different viewing conditions. For experiments to determine the distances at which ships disappeared, only one criterion was necessary – the vanishing point of the object. It was found that properly designed experiments performed on the Naval Camouflage Viewing Range were of great value in the elucidation of visibility problems and contributed significantly to the development of more effective camouflage designs.

The Germans, too, were engaged in detailed analysis of possible camouflage schemes for both naval and merchant surface ships, research which also involved the determination of accurate model viewing techniques. The Group MarRust, under the leadership of Dr A Kochs, carried out an extensive programme of model experiments to evaluate the possibilities of alternative painted concealment measures. The majority of the tests were carried out from 26 January 1943 by seven scientists supported by a photographic contractor, the Picture-Technics Department of the Universum Film Company, based in Berlin-Babelsberg Ufastadt. Both established and mooted camouflage colour designs were painted on 20cm-long ship stencils which were then set up on a synthesised seascape in a carefully constructed viewing gallery where they were studied and photographed by diffused 'daylight'. Particular studies were made of flicker camouflage concepts, that is dazzle, splinter, glimmer or twinkle painting schemes, all of which are collectively covered by the German term *flimmestarmung*.

Eighty experiments in total were conducted by the Group MarRust in the course of the research programme. Other effects examined included colour splotch systems, mock hull shapes on ships' sides (both light on dark and dark on light) hull length deception schemes and overall shape deception schemes. How much of this work led to practical application on vessels of the Kriegsmarine or on German mercantile auxiliaries is not known. The research team summarised the results of the experiments with two simple statements:

1 That concealment was a largely physiological effect
2 That deception was a pre-eminently psychological effect

In a sense they had confirmed, some 26 years after the event, the observations made by Loyd Ancile Jones and his Eastman Kodak staff, their World War I counterparts.

On reflection, camouflage in World War I had, it seems, been a practice expounded and pioneered by individuals – men of vision and creativity with a sense of purpose after the style of Isambard Kingdom Brunel and Charles Parsons. In contrast, World War II seemed to lack personalities and it is easy to form the impression that it was a war run by committees and anonymous War Departments. This could also be said to be true of those engaged in protective coloration work but, in fact, there were many vital and enterprising people making contributions to the development or greater understanding of the techniques involved in camouflage, men who, like their World War I predecessors, had been prominent artists, physicists or engineers in peacetime.

One such man was Alphonse E Schuil, a particularly gifted physicist who was employed

A good example of *flimmestarmung*, the German troopship *Goya* in a typical splinter camouflage. On 16 April 1945 the *Goya* was the victim of the second worst maritime disaster ever when she was torpedoed with the loss of more than 6,000 lives. This tragic incident and the unfortunate ship's name, commemorating the great Spanish painter, have a strangely fateful link, for Goya had produced a series of satirical etchings on the theme 'Disasters of War'. (*Arnold Kludas*)

It was suggested that the *Queen Elizabeth* and *Queen Mary* should be painted in Sir Peter Scott's Western Approaches Scheme. In the event they remained in neutral grey throughout the war although they were distinguished for the degaussing coils attached around their hulls: the *Queen Elizabeth*. (*Real Photos*)

The *Queen Mary*. Between them the *Queens* carried 1,243,538 troops during the course of their war service. (*Real Photos*)

by the GEC Research Laboratories until 1941, when he was attached to the staff of the Director of Training and Staff Duties Division, who had been made responsible for all sea-going camouflage. Schuil developed innovative methods for the long-range measurements of ship and sea brightnesses, using telephotometers, which permitted more accurate choices of paint colour and tone to be made to suit different applications. He also made significant contributions to the explanation of visual phenomena and the behaviour of light. Unfortunately, he was killed while engaged in camouflage observation trials off Freetown in 1943 when the ship he was on was torpedoed.

Another key personality involved in camouflage work in World War II was the artist and naturalist Peter Scott who, as a member of the Royal Naval Volunteer Reserve, was serving aboard destroyers escorting convoys in the Western Approaches. Scott was concerned with the tendency of ships to stand out as silhouettes against the night sky when viewed from the sea. Invited to devise a suitable camouflage which would diminish this effect, he developed a design, thereafter known as the Western Approaches Scheme, which provided a compromise between daytime and night-time concealment objectives. Upperworks and topsides were painted white while the lower hull was painted in shades of blue and green, the colours overlapping in a vividly irregular pattern. The scheme was adopted officially and widely used. It was even proposed for the Cunard liners *Queen Elizabeth* and *Queen Mary* which, sailing independently of convoys on troop crossings, were using their high speed as their prime means of protection from U-boat attack. In the event, however, they were not so painted. A derivative of the Western Approaches Scheme, which was used to make hull-down merchant ships less visible, involved the painting of funnel and mast tops white while the rest of the ship remained in neutral grey.

AMERICAN INTEREST in camouflage was rekindled in earnest in December 1941 when the Japanese attack on the Pacific Fleet at Pearl Harbor brought the United States into the war. There were two immediate outcomes which had a direct bearing on the contribution to the war effort of auxiliary vessels. In addition to taking up existing merchant passenger vessels as troop transports, a major new building programme was initiated to produce large numbers of purpose-built auxiliaries. Central to this effort were the eleven ships of the P2-S2-R2 class and the eight vessels of the P2-SE2-R1 class, all of which were designed around more or less conventional passenger-carrying hulls with a view to their being utilised for commercial employment after the end of the war.

Simultaneous with the launching of the Emergency Fleet building programme, the Navy Department's camouflage section was re-established in the Research and Development Branch of the Bureau of Ships, a new organisation formed in 1940 from a combination of the old Bureau of Engineering and Bureau of Construction and Repair. The new Camouflage Section was placed under the direction of Captain Henry A Ingram USN. Among the staff assembled in his unit were two key figures from the old, World War I Camouflage Section – Captain Charles Bittenger USNR and Everett Langley Warner, who contributed his services as a civilian consultant.

American naval ships and auxiliaries, which in peacetime had been painted uniform haze grey, were progressively repainted in other paint systems to suit the operational requirements of wartime. Initially, the measures adopted were based on low visibility objectives but, as the war progressed, confusion systems and other methods of deception were introduced to suit changing tactics and to respond to the differences in sea and light characteristics in diverse ocean areas. In spite of the relative absence of camouflage research between the wars, American camouflage techniques generally were already much more sophisticated than those practised in World War I. Effort was now

America entered World War II as a result of the infamous attack on the naval base at Pearl Harbor. Initially, her troop transport auxiliaries were, like their British counterparts, painted plain grey in Measures 1, 3, 13 and 14: here the Matson liner *Monterey*'s funnels still reveal the welded Ms that were part of her peacetime appearance. (*United States Coast Guard*)

The *West Point* (ex-*America*) (AP23) could accommodate 8,175 troops and had a range of 10,000 miles at 24 knots speed. (*United States National Archives*)

AP21, the *Wakefield* (ex-*Manhattan*). (*New York Daily News*)

concentrated on devising effects which would fully achieve both reduced visibility at longer ranges and optical confusion at shorter ranges.

Between late 1941 and 1945, the Section devised twenty-one basic camouflage measures which were adopted as official schemes while a large number of other techniques, which were not, in the event, approved for fleet application, were introduced experimentally. Detailed designs for each of the official measures were prepared for every vessel type to which they were applied. Where confusion schemes were applied to large classes of ships, and there was a danger that the class could be identified by the

Sister transport of the ***Wakefield***, the ***Mount Vernon*** (ex-***Washington***), AP22. (***United States National Archives***)

Another view of the ***Wakefield*** (ex-***Manhattan***), seen from the port stern quarter. Note the bank of Carley float rafts. (***World Ship Photo Library***)

camouflage pattern, several variations of the design were prepared to minimise this risk.

The Bureau of Ships Camouflage Section was among the first to realise that some sort of deck camouflage was required as a measure of protection for aerial observation. In collaboration with the Bureau of Aeronautics the problem was studied in great detail and two colour systems were devised which gave a close match to the ocean. Deck blue, a very dark blue, was applied as an even coating to some vessels, mainly aircraft carriers. For others, a lighter shade of the same colour was applied in combination with a light blue/grey colour.

Among the official measures introduced by the United States Navy's Camouflage Section during World War II were some innovative approaches to painted deception. Measures 12 and 22 (see Appendix 3) introduced a graded colouring scheme, typified by a strong contrast of colour above and below a level running the length of the hull, parallel to the waterline, which was designed to coincide with the distant horizon. In the right

The *Lafayette* (ex-*Normandie*) (AP53) would have been among the first United States' transports to put to sea in a patterned camouflage system. Even before her conversion was completed she had been repainted in what appears to be an early version of Measure 32 as this picture, taken at the height of her fateful fire, shows. (*United States National Archives*)

circumstances of light and atmosphere this subterfuge gave the impression that a ship was hull down, suggesting that it was further from the observer than it was.

Another stratagem, originally employed in World War I and now reintroduced, was the fake bow wave. Normally painted at the bow to suggest that a stationary vessel was under-way, it was also, occasionally, painted at the stern to create confusion as to where a ship's forward and aft ends really were and its true heading. Yet another trick that was revived was the painting of a silhouette of a different, smaller type of vessel on a ship's side, either as a disguise in itself or to give the illusion that a screening vessel lay between the target and its observer.

In practice these schemes were not wholly effective, particularly on ships that were under-way, although in favourable lighting and weather conditions they were of some benefit to ships in anchorages such as the invasion fleets assembled for Operation Torch, Operation Overlord and other amphibious landings. Generally, though, schemes of this type were of dubious value and on ships seen end on or at acute angles from the bow to stern they were little use at all. When similar approaches to visual deception had been tried out in World War I, for the most part they had been abandoned as ineffective, in spite of the incorporation of some quite clever refinements. One of these had involved the

The most widely used American protective colouring scheme was Measure 22, a graded system using haze grey and navy blue: the *Hermitage* (AP54), the former *Conte Biancamano,* an Italian liner taken over following the United States' entry into the war. (*United States National Archives*)

Another Matson liner, the *Mariposa.* (*World Ship Photo Library*)

The *Wakefield* suffered a serious fire in mid-Atlantic in September 1942, but against all the odds the ship was recovered and rebuilt. When she re-emerged, in April 1944, she had lost her promenade deck and her close resemblance to her sister, the *Mount Vernon.* (*United States Coast Guard*)

The break of colour, characteristic of Measure 22, is clearly shown in this view of the *Lejeune* (ex-*Windhuk*) (AP74). (*United States National Archives*)

Soon after returning to auxiliary service, the *Wakefield* too was repainted in Measure 22. See how well the level separating the two shades of paint merges with the horizon. (*United States National Archives*)

A similar experience to that of the *Wakefield* befell the British troopship *Georgic* which was bombed and set on fire at Port Tewfik, Suez on 14 July 1941. She is seen here, after her lengthy and expensive restoration, minus one funnel. She also no longer bore any resemblance to her sister ship, the *Britannic*. (*J McRoberts*)

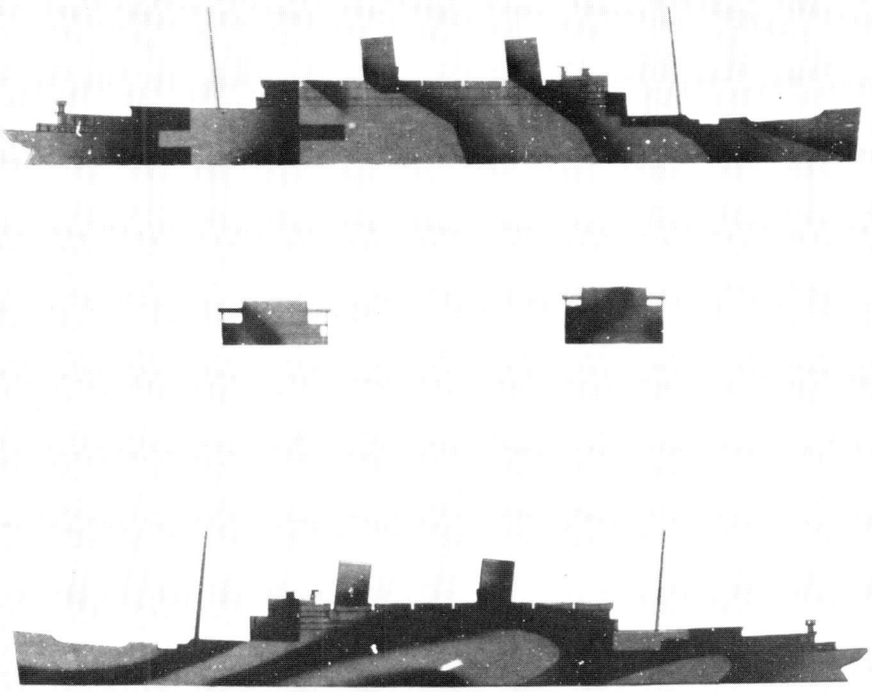

It had been intended by the US Navy that both the ***Wakefield*** and ***Mount Vernon*** should be painted in a different, distinctive colour system – Measure 32 in design 1T. Measure 32, which was designed primarily as an anti-submarine camouflage, was also the preferred scheme for vessels that were likely to be detected by enemy radar. ***(United States Naval Historical Center)***

The *Westpoint* was repainted in Measure 33, a scheme clearly revealed in this aerial photograph dating from 6 June 1943. *(United States National Archives)*

welding of angle iron on a ship's side at the point where the bow of the fake ship intersected the waterline, so that, when under-way, the decoy had a genuine bow wave.

The problems encountered with deception techniques such as these, which were intended to give false inpressions rather than to conceal, were similar to those experienced with virtually all other camouflage schemes. All had merits in certain conditions but were often valueless in others, reinforcing the quest for a truly universal, self-adjusting camouflage system or material. In the absence of such a highly desirable commodity, camouflage technicians were compelled to weigh up the advantages and disadvantages of different schemes, and their effectiveness in a variety of circumstances, against the costs of implementing and maintaining them, before deciding which to adopt and which to abandon. It was often for this reason that, in World War II, auxiliaries and naval vessels were painted in either simple low visibility neutral colours or in light interference patterns rather than in anything more complex.

As senior partners in the Alliance, the British and American authorities closely coordinated their camouflage activities throughout the war. By this time the Ministry of War Transport was responsible for all British troopships and other non-naval auxiliaries, having been formed in 1941 from the existing Ministry of Shipping and Ministry of Transport. The Ministry of War Transport adopted the camouflage measures agreed with the Admiralty which had been developed by the Admiralty's camouflage research centre and its Home Office counterpart. These schemes were increasingly influenced by the coordinated approach to camouflage matters pursued by the Allies.

By late 1942 the list of standard Admiralty camouflage colours already contained many of the standard colours of the United States Navy and, as the war progressed, others were added. When operational requirements demanded it and Royal Navy vessels were called upon to operate closely with American warships, such as when the British Pacific Fleet was formed into Task Force 57 in the closing months of the war, the British vessels adopted American camouflage practice. It should be stressed, however, that there is no known instance of British passenger ship auxiliaries being required to adopt alternative colourings in like manner.

Nor, it should be stated, was the coordination between the USA and Britain on camouflage matters one-sided. In October 1944, a major evaluation exercise involving all Admiralty and United States Navy camouflage measures was undertaken by the Bureau of Ships at Washington and at Bethesda, Maryland, in order to determine conclusively which schemes were the most effective. Further tests were carried out in April 1945 at Miami and Fort Lauderdale, Florida. The intention was to dispense with those schemes of dubious or limited value, regardless of their origin, and concentrate collaboratively on those that worked well or best. However, by the time Lieutenant Lewis W Rubenstein completed the report on these trials, the war was already drawing to a close and the

Though she is not a passenger ship conversion, the *Lamont*, serving as an Infantry Landing Ship, provides an example of the 'hopeful hoax', the fake hull painted on a ship's side in lighter or darker colours. (*Imperial War Museum*)

Wearing camouflage colours akin to the American Measure 32, the *Glen Gyle* enters the Grand Harbour, Valletta, Malta. (*Imperial War Museum*)

significance of its contents was no longer considered vital.

Long before then, the submarine war in the Atlantic had been causing great concern, just as it had done in 1917. This particular aspect of the maritime conflict was characterised by move and counter-move as first one side and then the other sought to gain the upper-hand. The wolf pack tactics of the German U-boats dominated the early phases of the battle, the convoy system adopted by the Admiralty unwittingly aiding, to some extent, this policy. Escorts were then in short supply, so by drawing these guardians away from their charges the U-boats were able to concentrate their attack against the unprotected merchantmen, largely unhindered and in large numbers. While the building programme for new escorts was stepped up, the British also turned to electronic means, with devices like Asdic and Huff Duff, and improved undersea weapons, such as Hedgehog and Squid, to redress the tactical balance. The most significant anti-submarine warfare tactic adopted by the Allies was the provision of air cover for the convoys, a move which resulted in many merchant auxiliaries becoming the protectors of their fellow vessels.

The first mercantile auxiliary aircraft carriers were the CAM-ships (Catapult Armed Merchant ships), forerunners to the later MAC-ships (Merchant Aircraft Carriers), on which full, permanent flight decks were erected over the cargo holds. This allowed the ships to serve, simultaneously, as cargo carriers and convoy air patrol bases. A total of nineteen of these vessels were completed and they in turn were followed by the true mercantile escort carriers of which over a hundred were built.

Although their modified appearance owed more to functional requirements rather than camouflage objectives, it is fitting to refer here to the wartime conversions of certain passenger liners into aircraft carriers. The very first had been the Royal Navy's

The Nippon Yusen Kaisha passenger liner *Yawata Maru*, one of a class of three vessels converted into auxiliary carriers during World War II. As a 'flat top' she was renamed *Unyo*. (*Nippon Yusen Kaisha*)

Two much bigger *NYK* ships were converted into fleet carriers. This is the *Hiyo* (ex-*Izumo Maru*) which was sunk during the Battle of the Philippine Sea in July 1944. As a navy ship she was painted dark green overall. (*Fujiphotos*)

The very first passenger ship ever to be converted into an aircraft carrier, the former Cunard liner *Campania* seen in dazzle colours during World War I. (*Imperial War Museum*)

Campania and *Argus* (ex-*Conte Rosso*), rebuilt in World War I. Although these had been permanent fleet conversions, they demonstrated early on the suitability of such merchant ships for rapid adaptation to this role. Between the wars, the restrictions imposed by naval treaties on the numbers of new warships each country could build led to the subsidised construction of passenger liners incorporating design features which would aid speedy conversion into aircraft carriers during wartime. In a sense, therefore, these vessels were the twentieth-century equivalent of the auxiliary cruisers of the late Victorian and Edwardian eras.

The Washington Naval Treaty imposed tighter restrictions on the Imperial Japanese Navy than on either the Royal Navy or the United States Navy, so that Japan in particular, resorted to this approach for the reinforcement of her fleet. By the time of the attack on Pearl Harbor, Japan had no fewer than seven passenger liners in the process of being converted or available for conversion into aircraft carriers. But she was not the only country to opt for the adaptation of passenger carrying vessels into auxiliary carriers. When war broke out Italy undertook the reconstruction of the liners *Roma* and *Augustus* into the aircraft carriers *Aquila* and *Sparviero*, respectively, and gave serious consideration to doing likewise with the express steamers *Rex* and *Conte Di Savoia*. Germany, too, prepared designs for rebuilding the Norddeutscher Lloyd giant *Europa* into an aircraft carrier as did the Americans with the French record-breaker *Normandie* which had been interned in New York since 1939. Germany also commenced the reconstruction of the smaller liners *Potsdam* and *Gneisenau*. Their consort, the *Scharnhorst*, had already undergone a similar conversion for the Japanese. These plans, however, were never concluded and Britain was the only other nation to convert fully a passenger liner into an auxiliary carrier, this being the Union Castle Line's *Pretoria Castle*.

This increased utilisation of passenger liners as aircraft carriers serves as a good example of the greater specialisation in the auxiliary roles undertaken by passenger ships in World War II compared with World War I, and all these roles depended in part on camouflage schemes for protection. For both American and British passenger ships there was increased diversification in the naval duties for which they were adapted. The *Llangibby Castle* and *Corfu*, for instance, were employed along with many other liners as infantry landing ships in support of invasions forces. The *Wolfe* (ex-*Montcalm*) became a submarine and destroyer depot ship while the *Artifex* (ex-*Aurania*) and her sister ships

The *Aquila* (ex-*Roma*), Italian aircraft carrier, seen at Genoa following salvage at the end of World War II and before the decision was made that she should be demolished. (*Imperial War Museum*)

The Italia Line passenger ship *Roma* seen prior to the drastic reconstruction which transformed her into an aircraft carrier. Comparing this with the picture on page 125, it is hard to believe that both photographs show the same ship. (*L L von Münching*)

HMS *Pretoria Castle*, converted Union Castle Line mail ship, painted in a version of the Admiralty Intermediate Disruptive Pattern. (*Imperial War Museum*)

The Infantry Landing Ship *Tegelberg* sailing in a 500-ship convoy, containing numerous other passenger ship auxiliaries, transporting troops for the landings in French North Africa in November 1942. (*Imperial War Museum*)

A selection of other passenger vessels converted into large Infantry Landing Ships:
Union Castle's *Llangibby Castle*. She was later repainted in an Admiralty Disruptive Pattern. (*Imperial War Museum*)

The *Monowai* returning to Portsmouth from a rehearsal of the D-Day invasion that took place in the Channel, off the Isle of Wight, between 24 and 28 April 1944. (*Imperial War Museum*)

HMS *Wolfe* (ex-*Montcalm*), Submarine and Destroyer Depot Ship, apparently wearing a derivative of the Admiralty Standard Scheme. (*Imperial War Museum*)

The British India liner *Keren*. (*Imperial War Museum*)

The Royal Mail Line's *Asturias*, seen postwar but still serving as a troopship and emigrant carrier. Like her sister ship *Alcantara*, she had her forward funnel removed during the war whereas P&O's *Ranchi, Rajputana* and *Rawalpindi* had their aft funnels removed. (*Richard de Kerbrech*)

The Base Repair Ship *Artifex* (ex-*Aurania*) in a distinctive camouflage colour system, probably a variant of the Admiralty Intermediate Disruptive Pattern. (*Imperial War Museum*)

Similarly painted, the *Corfu* seen as an Armed Merchant Cruiser in May 1943. Note the Kingfisher catapult aircraft stowed just forward of the crane. (*Imperial War Museum*)

The former Panama Railroad Company's *Ancon* served as an Amphibious Command and Headquarters Ship during the major seaborne landings of World War II, a role which necessitated the erection of huge radio antennae aboard her. She is seen here, in Measure 32, departing for the Pacific theatre on 21 December 1944. (*United States Naval Historical Center*)

Ausonia, *Alaunia* and *Antonia*, as the *Wayland*, were acquired for permanent retention by the Royal Navy as repair ships. A similar situation prevailed in the United States where the Panama Railroad Company's passenger ship *Ancon* was equipped for a unique auxiliary role, serving as an amphibious command and headquarters ship during the landings at Salerno, Normandy and Okinawa.

The majority of these auxiliaries, as navy ships, were camouflaged in naval schemes. Many of them were also treated with a measure of dynamic camouflage in order to make identification difficult. A string of British ships had one or more of their funnels removed to alter their profile, among them the *Queen of Bermuda*, *Alcantara* and *Asturias*, the *Corfu*, *Chitral* and other units of P&O's R and S classes. The *Cathay*, for a while, sported only one and a half funnels.

The *Robert Ley* laid up as an accommodation ship at Pillau in the eastern Baltic. Apart from camouflage colours on her side, she has nets draped over her funnel. (*L L von Münching*)

GERMANY, TOO, ADAPTED her passenger ship auxiliaries to a variety of roles but this had more to do with the immediate exigencies of war than to fulfil some master plan designed to achieve victory. Increasingly, following the United States' entry into the war, air raids wreaked greater and greater havoc further into Germany's heartland. Vital U-boat personnel stationed at German Baltic ports came within the range of allied aircraft and had to be moved further along the Baltic to bases in occupied Poland. Shortages of suitable shore accommodation demanded that ships be made available instead for living quarters and many of the liners originally adapted for service as hospital ships were now reconverted to act as floating barracks.

Gradually, though, even these remote harbours became vulnerable to aerial attack. The destruction of the *Stuttgart* at Gdynia on 9 October 1943, with the loss of many naval officers and seamen, was a frighteningly graphic demonstration of what ultimately lay in store for other German accommodation ships. Some were moved even further along the Baltic coastline to Pillau, East Prussia, (now Baltiysk in the Soviet Union) where attempts were made to disguise them against attack from the air. The former Strength Through Joy flagship *Robert Ley* was painted in a typical military disruption pattern and had nets spread over her funnels and superstructure to help her blend in with the background landscape. Apparently, as allied air supremacy was also established in the Mediterranean, some Italian liners holed up in lagoons and obscure anchorages along the Adriatic coast were given similar treatment. At the time she was attacked at Mallamocco, near Venice, on 11 September 1943, the *Conte di Savoia* was reported to have been disguised as an island.

Hardly had the remnants of the German passenger fleet been moved to new locations than German land forces were forced to retreat in the face of the advancing Red Army and the ships were diverted to a new role, evacuating civilians and military personnel to the West. In January 1945, as the Russians were threatening to cross the Vistula Peninsula and encircle the Gulf of Danzig, Grand Admiral Dönitz hatched a plan for the evacuation of German citizens trapped in the region. Awe-inspiring in its scale, it was codenamed Operation Hannibal. The fleet that was assembled for the operation was immense, dwarfing that which Britain had hurriedly gathered together for the relief of Dunkirk some four and a half years earlier. In all, 509 ships were engaged to undertake mercy voyages, of which twenty-four were former German passenger ships:

The Hamburg Sud Amerika liner *Monte Rosa* in a striking zebra-striped camouflage scheme. She was also used as an accommodation ship in the Baltic. (*Hamburg Sud-Amerika*)

Towards the end of the war the *Ancon* was repainted overall grey, in Measure 14. (*United States Naval Historical Center*)

As RAF Beaufighter warplanes swoop down to attack the Italian flagship *Rex*, in vain seeking refuge close to Italy's Adriatic coastline, their first shots are wide of the target. The liner's colours appear to have been little altered apart from her funnels which have been painted white or light grey. (*Imperial War Museum*)

Antonio Delfino	Hamburg Sud Amerika
Berlin	Norddeutscher Lloyd
Cap Arcona	Hamburg Sud Amerika
Der Deutsche	Deutsche Arbeitsfront
Deutschland	Hamburg Amerika
General San Martin	Hamburg Sud Amerika
Hamburg	Hamburg Amerika
Hansa	Hamburg Amerika
Iberia	Hamburg Amerika
Monte Olivia	Hamburg Sud Amerika
Monte Rosa	Hamburg Sud Amerika
New York	Hamburg Amerika
Oceana	Deutsche Arbeitsfront
Oranjefontein	United Netherlands SS Co (captured)
Potsdam	Norddeutscher Lloyd
Pretoria	Deutsche Ost Afrika
Robert Ley	Deutsche Arbeitsfront
Steuben	Norddeutscher Lloyd
Ubena	Deutsche Ost Afrika
Usambara	Deutsche Ost Afrika
Wadai	Deutsche Ost Afrika
Wangoni	Deutsche Ost Afrika
Wilhelm Gustloff	Deutsche Arbeitsfront
Winrich von Kniprode	Hamburg Amerika

The troopship *Sabaudia* (ex-*Stockholm*) at the CRDA shipyard in Monfalcone. It is understood that she was never used in this role because of the risk of aerial attack. The Swedish Amerika Line colours in which she was originally completed have been overpainted with a dark shade on the hull and a lighter colour on her funnels. (*Aldo Fraccaroli*)

The *Wilhelm Gustloff* prewar, in Hamburg harbour. She was sunk on 31 January 1945 with record loss of life, an ill omen for Operation Hannibal which had hardly begun by that date. (*L L von Münching*)

The losses were staggering as ships fell prey to British or American aircraft, Russian submarines or even to mines that had been laid in the approaches to the ports at Kiel, Lubeck, Peenemunde and Swinemunde. Despite the fact that the exercise clocked up three of the most costly sinkings ever – the *Wilhelm Gustloff* on 30 January 1945 with over 7,000 lives lost, the *Steuben* on 10 February 1945 with more than 3,000 casualties and the *Goya* on 16 April 1945 with a further 6,000 deaths – Operation Hannibal was judged to be a success, ensuring freedom, in the West, for more than two million people.

One aspect of the operation which, nevertheless, raises questions was the failure of the German authorities to seek the immunity of diplomatic status for certain vessels to convey only civilian passengers. Although timing was of the essence and it was known that negotiations on these matters could become quite protracted, little effort was apparently made to separate U-boats and military personnel from other passenger categories, despite the relatively low numbers of the former group compared with the total number evacuated. In consequence, all vessels involved in the operation were rendered legitimate targets, resulting in untold suffering being inflicted on civilians.

The Japanese seaplane carrier *Sagara Maru* sporting dazzle camouflage design by the Kure Navy Yard. It was the first attempt at a protective colouring design for a ship operating in the area of the Indian Ocean near Malaya and Burma. It was described as having been 'very successful'. (*Imperial War Museum*)

The AMC *Aikoku Maru* in another dazzle design from the Kure Navy Yard. The *Aikoku Maru* with her sister, the *Hokoku Maru*, were involved in a surface engagement with the Dutch tanker *Onda* and the Indian frigate *Bengal* in the Indian Ocean on 11 November 1942. The *Hokoku Maru* was sunk by a single 4in shell while the *Aikoku Maru* was seriously damaged. The two allied vessels survived the encounter. (*Imperial War Museum*)

Lacking any particular status, the motley collection of war-worn and neglected passenger ships that participated in Operation Hannibal exhibited no distinct colour scheme, having been more or less sent to sea in whatever state they were found. Engine failures and breakdowns were commonplace and few survived to see the war's end.

The termination of hostilities in Europe on 8 May 1945 and in the Far East on 2 September 1945, permitted the Allies to gain access to enemy wartime records including papers and reports on camouflage practices. The key activities of the German camouflage researchers have already been described and the Japanese were discovered to have been similarly active in the development of concealment and confusion schemes. Here the momentum of research rested mainly with the shipyards and it was largely left to them, independently, to conceive and implement designs that would provide a measure of disguise or deception. In this the Kure Navy Yard was especially prominent. The very first Japanese camouflage scheme, applied to the converted seaplane carrier *Sagara Maru*, originated in the yard's design offices. In general, the Japanese favoured splinter or pseudo-dazzle patterns for their merchant auxiliaries but as the course of the war turned against them and their ships were compelled increasingly to run the gauntlet of an ever growing fleet of hostile submarines even, in the end, in their home waters, so the value of these systems was lost. Apart from this, the urgent need to keep ships at sea to ferry in vital raw materials and foodstuffs, coupled with the diminishing resources at the country's disposal, particularly for the manufacture of paints, resulted in declining maintenance of those paint schemes that were applied.

It is doubtful, given the weight of the military offensive rallied against Japan, whether the existence or absence of camouflage on her naval ships and merchant auxiliaries would have made any difference to the total decimation of her fleet. The scale of these losses in terms of passenger ships can be conveyed by one simple statistic – at the war's end only one major unit from Japan's vast prewar passenger fleet remained afloat. This was the *Hikawa Maru* which probably owed her good fortune more to the fact that she was a hospital ship than to anything else.

The *Hokoku Maru*. At the time of her sinking she was also acting as a Submarine Storeship, carrying ammunition, petrol, and oxygen torpedoes. It is believed that the *Bengal*'s single shell hit struck her ammunition store which would account for her rapid demise. (*Imperial War Museum*)

The *Europa*'s six years of enforced immobility came to an end when the American authorities moved her across the River Weser to drydock for inspection and repainting. Afterwards she sailed to the United States where she was refitted as a troop transport. She is seen still wearing the dazzle colouring which had been applied for her participation in Operation Sealion. (*Imperial War Museum*)

The United States troopship *Europa* (AP177) completing her fitting out at the Todd Shipyard, Brooklyn, following which she was used to repatriate American servicemen from Europe. (*L L von Münching*)

With the ending of hostilities, many liners were returned to their owners for refurbishment for continued commercial service: the *Queen of Bermuda* in dock at Liverpool early in 1947. (*World Ship Photo Library*)

The *Aquitania* in Southampton Water on 31 May 1946. Though she retains her wartime grey hull, her funnels have been repainted in their commercial colours. (*CPL*)

Another *Monterey*, the former *Puerto Rico*, refitting in October 1948. (*World Ship Photo Library*)

The *John Ericson* (ex-*Kungsholm*) partially refitted. Her hull colours are still those of her troopship days but her funnels are painted in an unrecognisable company livery. Following a fire, she finally returned to service under the Home Line's banner as the *Italia*. (*World Ship Photo Library*)

A well-known photograph which shows the transition process as wartime auxiliaries were restored for civilian duties. The *Queen Elizabeth*, on the left, has been converted already while the *Queen Mary* still wears her wartime colours apart from on her funnels. (*Southern Newspapers*)

AS HAD BEEN THE CASE following the end of World War I, passenger ship auxiliaries continued with emergency duties long after the end of the war. Trooping and repatriation work continued for many well into 1947; others were tied up for war bride and immigrant voyages, all of which resulted in an array of odd colour schemes as ships partially reverted to their commercial livery.

By the end of the 1940s the global shipping situation had largely settled back to its

prewar pattern. The majority of commandeered passenger vessels had returned to their line services and peacetime trooping had been resumed once again by the Ministry of Transport on behalf of the United Kingdom and by the Military Sea Transportation Service for the United States. America's industrial prowess had flowered during World War II and her political and military influence had spread throughout the world. Her numerous overseas bases and her commitments to the NATO and SEATO military treaties necessitated the movement of large numbers of troops and the distinctive P2

While many ships were returned to commercial service soon after the end of the war, others were retained on military duties for considerably longer: Anchor Line's *Cameronia* on 11 June 1947. (*Michael Cassar*).

The *Washington* (ex-*Mount Vernon*, ex-*Washington*) at Southampton in the late 1940s. As it turned out, she was never fully restored to her prewar glory. (*Tom Rayner*)

The *Empress of Australia* (ex-*Tirpitz*), herself a prize from World War I, still painted navy grey on 19 April 1948. (*Michael Cassar*)

troopships became a common sight on the world's sealanes throughout the 1950s and early 1960s.

The Ministry of Transport also had an enduring commitment to transport British troops overseas for as long as the government maintained its 'east of Suez' policy. The older Bibby and British India vessels were dispensed with. In their place captured German liners were converted into dedicated troop carriers while two new ships, the *Nevasa* and *Oxfordshire*, were ordered from Barclay, Curle & Company and the Fairfield Shipbuilding Company respectively.

The Suez Crisis in Autumn 1956 saw some of these older troop carriers switched

P&O's *Strathnaver* at Valletta on 15 May 1948. (*Michael Cassar*)

The *Empire Orwell* (ex-*Pretoria*), rebuilt as a purpose-designed Ministry of Transport troopship. During the war the *Pretoria* had served as a German naval hospital ship. (*Tom Rayner*)

briefly to active trooping again. Also, the French passenger liner *La Marseillaise* was temporarily converted into a hospital ship for the operation. It seemed that there was still a future for converted passenger ships in support of a military campaign.

Nevertheless, the writing was on the wall and just as the burgeoning civil aviation industry spelt disaster for ocean passenger liner services, so too, the development of long-range military transport aircraft with inflight refuelling capability, meant the end for the transportation of troops by ship. After only eight seasons the new troopships made their last troop voyages, the *Nevasa* in October 1962 and the *Oxfordshire* in December of the same year. Seemingly, after 110 years, the long era of the engine-driven passenger

Another former German liner converted into an MoT troopship, the *Empire Fowey* (ex-*Potsdam*). (*Tom Rayner*)

Postwar the *El Nil* also joined the Ministry of Transport fleet. This picture was taken on 10 July 1950. (*Tom Rayner*)

After World War II the vast fleet of American P2 transports was operated by the Military Sea Transportation Service: the *General H W Butner* of the P2-S2-R2 class, still in US Navy colours. (*Tom Rayner*)

ship auxiliary had closed. But who then could have imagined the events that were to unfold in 1982 in the Falkland Islands, the farthest outpost dependent on Britain for its security?

Suddenly catapulted into a conflict necessitating the movement of large numbers of troops some 7,000 miles away against a much more conveniently disposed adversary, a major policy rethink was thrust upon defence chiefs, for the islands were already occupied and no other friendly base was available in the area for the conveyance of troops by air. Even if one had been, the distance involved was beyond the range of the most powerful transport planes. The availability of Ascension Island as a refuelling point was of no help, for the aircraft would still have had insufficient fuel for the return flight, besides which a piecemeal, unsupported airborne invasion could have proved disastrous. There

The *General Maurice Rose* (T-AP-126) of the P2-SE2-R1 class in MSTS colours. (*Tom Rayner*)

During the late 1940s and early 1950s the *Pasteur* continued to serve as a French Government troopship carrying soldiers to the fighting in Vietnam, then part of French Indo-China. (*Photo Marine*)

The fifth and last *Maine*, the former *Leonardo da Vinci*, an Italian passenger liner seized during World War II. The *Maine* served as a hospital ship during the Korean War. Note how the cross on one funnel is painted while that on the other funnel is a rig for night time illumination. (*Maritime Photo Library*)

Britain's final pair of Ministry of Transport troopships: the *Nevasa* ... (*Tom Rayner*)

... and *Oxfordshire*. (*Tom Rayner*)

During the Suez Crisis the Messageries Maritimes liner *La Marseillaise* was taken up briefly for hospital ship service. She made only three round voyages between Marseilles and Port Said, commencing 1 October 1956 and terminating 26 December 1956. (*Cie Générale Maritime*)

En route to the Falklands. Scenes aboard the *Queen Elizabeth* 2: exercises for the troops on the aft sun deck. (*Brian Atkinson*)

Sea King helicopters operating from the aft helipad. (*Brian Atkinson*)

The *Canberra* with the *Queen Elizabeth* 2 at Cumberland Bay, South Georgia on 25 May 1982. (*Imperial War Museum*)

The British India educational cruise ship *Uganda* in hospital ship guise during the Falklands Campaign, seen at sea with the Argentine hospital ship *Bahia Paraiso*. (*Imperial War Museum*)

The ***Raffaello***, on the left, and the ***Michelangelo*** were sold to the Imperial Iranian Navy in 1976 for service as naval accommodation ships based at Bushire and Bandar Abbas. (***Italia SpA***)

was only one solution – the revival of trooping by sea using requisitioned merchant passenger ships. Under Operation Corporate some six large passenger ships were therefore taken over for the duration, part of a fleet which included fifty merchant ships in all. The *Queen Elizabeth 2*, *Canberra* (thereafter known somewhat unflatteringly as the Great White Whale), *Rangatira* and the North Sea ferries *Norland* and *Norstar* were

Model of the ***United States*** as a hospital ship as projected for the Rapid Deployment Force. Note the large helicopter pad aft and smaller one forward. (***David W Taylor Research Center, Bethesda, US Navy Dept, Naval Sea Systems Command***)

The *United States* was not, in the event, rebuilt as a hospital ship. Instead she continued in lay up at Norfolk, Virginia. Appropriately, in a book concerned with passenger ship colouring, it is interesting to note how, as her scheme in this May 1980 picture shows, the ship's 1969 refit was abruptly ended when lost subsidies forced the United States Lines to prematurely retire her. (*Norfolk Shipbuilding & Drydock Corp*)

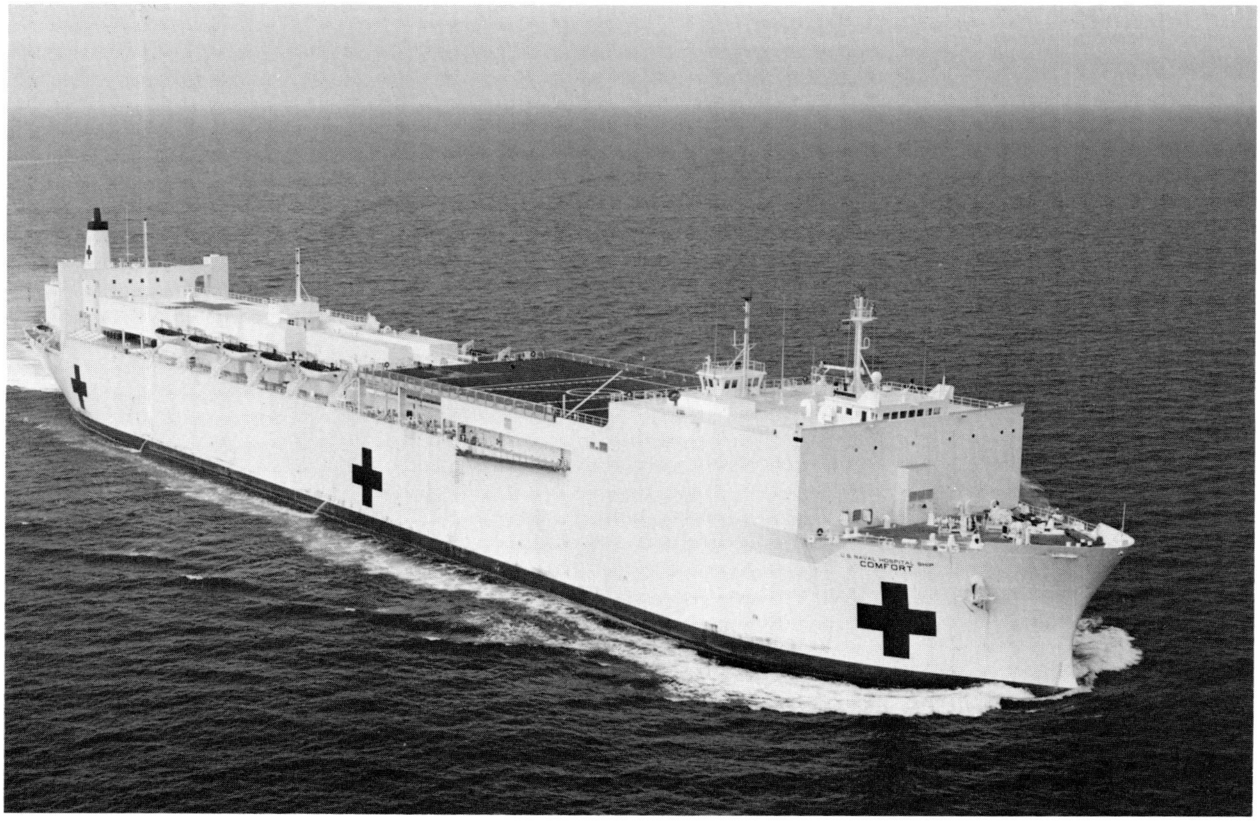

In place of the *United States*, the US Navy took up instead the redundant oil tankers *Rose City* and *Worth* which were converted into the hospital ships *Comfort* seen here, and *Mercy*. (*National Steel & Shipbuilding Co*)

The troopships return from the Falklands Campaign, the end of auxiliary service for the *Queen Elizabeth* 2 and ...
(*Peter Alford*)

used as troopships while the British India schools cruise ship *Uganda* became a hospital ship.

In fact, this re-emergence of the passenger ship auxiliary had not occurred exlusively in Britain. Six years earlier the Imperial Iranian Navy had bought the Italia Line sisters *Raffaello* and *Michelangelo*, albeit for a static role, as crew accommodation ships based at Bandar Abbas and Bushire.

More recently, the United States Navy had announced its intentions to refit the Atlantic Blue Riband holder *United States* as a hospital ship/troop transport to be attached to the Military Sealift Command's Rapid Deployment Force. This was very fitting in that the *United States* was the only one of the large, express passenger liners to be originally designed as a fast troopship and fitted out for commercial passenger carrying operations rather than the other way round. It was this reversal of practice which brought about her downfall as a passenger liner. The immense power plant installed aboard her to provide a maximum speed, reportedly as high as 38.32 knots for military purposes, also denied her a large amount of valuable revenue-earning accommodation space. She was only able to show a profit under the United States Lines' banner for as long as sizeable operating subsidies propped up her balance sheet. When these were terminated in 1969 she was laid up as commercially unviable.

The first announcement of plans for the *United States* came in the winter of 1980 when it was revealed by the Assistant Secretary of Defense that, at a cost of US$230 million, she would be converted into a 2,000 bed mobile hospital with all associated facilities. By the spring of 1981 the cost of the conversion had been re-estimated at US$395 million. Nevertheless, the scheme proceeded and detailed revelations that summer showed the *United States* in full hospital ship rig. Structurally, a full helicopter landing pad was to be constructed aft and other modifications were to be made in the region of her foredeck. In the end the scheme faltered, not surprisingly, on cost grounds and the *United States'* new lease of life never materialised. In her place the supertankers *Rose City* and *Worth* were

... the *Canberra*. Almost certainly, this was also the last time that ocean passenger ships would be taken up for auxiliary war service. (*Peter Alford*)

taken up, re-emerging as the hospital ships *Comfort* and *Mercy* respectively.

As to the auxiliaries that formed part of the Falklands Task Force, only one, the *Uganda*, was repainted and this was into the regulation hospital ship colours stipulated by the Geneva Convention. No colour obscuration or concealment was even considered for the converted troopships for the ability of modern missile systems to seek out targets electronically, over the horizon if necessary, rendered visual camouflage largely irrelevant.

In a sense, this simple statement of fact brings this book to a close, although in truth, the pursuit of camouflage continues, albeit by electronic rather than painted methods. Back in 1945 the British and Canadians were experimenting with 'illuminated' camouflage by which, using floodlights attached to outriggers and sophisticated light metering systems, ships could be lit up to a brightness level equivalent to the intensity of the skylight beyond them and hence be concealed in their background. In practice the equipment was cumbersome and prone to damage in a heaving seaway so the scheme was abandoned as impractical. However, the principle involved was much the same as that of modern electronic disguise.

Techniques of generating false radio or radar emissions that match those of other sources, even the enemy's own, to act as decoys for potential targets are well enough known. More recently the practice of emitting infra-red transmissions corresponding to those of the ambient environment has permitted military vehicles to 'hide' from the sensory devices of enemy tracking equipment.

In modern construction materials, such as the advanced composites from which the American Stealth bomber has been built, the subterfuge of 'invisibility' is achieved in a different way. The characteristics of these materials permit the virtual elimination of an electronic signature resulting in near absence of a radar screen image. Coupled with extreme high speed and low altitude beneath-radar manoeuvrability, such vehicles can operate unseen.

Paints also continue to play a part in space age camouflage. Unlike the coloured coatings of the past, whose concealment value depended on tone, reflectivity and pigment, the vital characteristic of modern protective coatings is their ability to absorb radio frequency energy so that the word concealment is given a whole new meaning.

This, in very simple terms, is the state of the art as far as modern camouflage technology is concerned. Whether any of these developments will ever be applied to future passenger ship auxiliaries is highly unlikely. While on the one hand their commissioning and conversion would stimulate great public interest, as it did at the time of the Falklands Campaign, it could only be in association with a state of hostility or conflict, a situation that would be both undesirable and unwelcome.

Appendices

Appendix 1

Eastman Kodak, USA
Approved Interim Camouflage Schemes
World War 1

The following schemes are listed in alphabetical order.

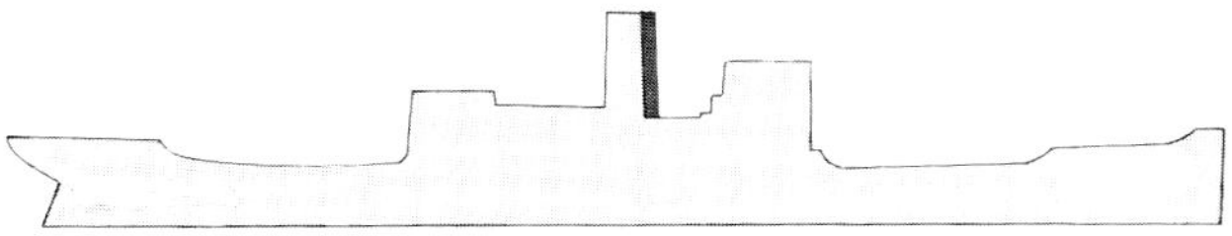

1 Brush countershading low visibility scheme.
Colours:
black and dark greys applied to exposed surfaces; white and light greys applied to shaded areas under deck structures.

2 Herzog low visibility disruptive scheme.
Colours:
blue and green applied in arcs and curves over a violet/grey base.

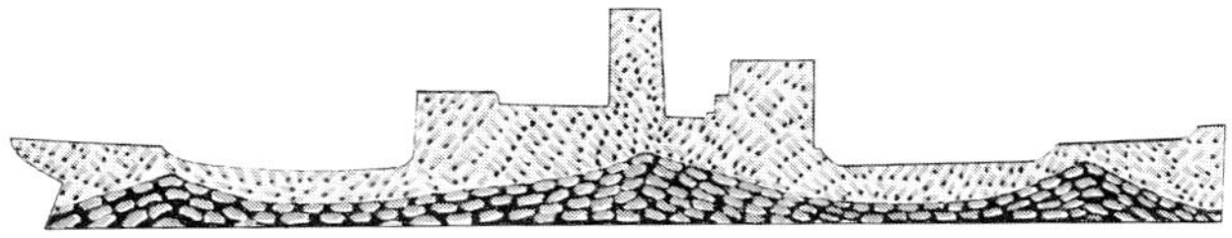

3 Mackay low visibility scheme.
Colours:
red, green and violet – two of the colours applied in speckles over the third colour, painted as a base.

4 Mackay low visibility disruptive scheme.
Colours:
green, orange and white applied in bold, undulating shapes above an area of solid blue along the lower hull above the waterline.

5 Toch low visibility disruptive scheme.
Colours:
light blue-grey, dark blue-grey, dark green and light pink-purple applied in an abstract fashion with the darker colours concentrated near the waterline.

6 Warner dazzle scheme.
Colours:
red, blue, green and white or contrasting greys applied in strongly-contrasting, large, irregular patterns.

7 Watson dazzle scheme.
Colours:
a range of dark and light colours – three different shades used in each application, painted in bold, regular geometric patterns.

On the recommendation of the Camouflage Research Center at Eastman Kodak, the US Navy's Bureau of Construction and Repair finally adopted a dazzle painting system which was very similar to that of the British Admiralty.

Appendix 2

Admiralty Standard Camouflage Colours
Disruptive Patterns and Standard Schemes
World War II

1. Standard Camouflage Colours
The standardisation of these colours was established by the Admiralty Paint Research Station at Teddington, Middlesex, by colorimetric measurements, for colour, photometric measurements, for brightness, and reflectivity measurements.

Nominal Colour	*Designation*	*Pattern No.*	
dark grey	Home Fleet Grey 507A	1	Standard
light grey	Mediterranean Grey 507C	2	Admiralty colours
black	MS1	3	
dark grey	MS2	4	
mid-grey	MS3	5	Admiralty
light mid-grey	MS4	6	camouflage colours
light grey	MS4A	7	
dark blue	B5	8	
mid-grey/blue	B6	9	

Nominal Colour	*Designation*	*Pattern No.*	
grey/pink	Mountbatten Pink	10	Special colours –
light blue	Peter Scott Blue	11	Western Approaches
black/grey	MSD	12	Admiralty merchant
mid-grey	MSS	13	ship colours
dark grey	US Dark Grey	14	
dark mid-grey	US Ocean Grey	15	
mid-grey/blue	US Haze Grey	16	
light grey	US Light Grey	17	United States Navy
v.dark blue/black	US Deck Blue	18	Colours
dark grey/blue	US Sea Blue	19	
black	Black	20	
white	White	21	

This list dates from October 1942. As the war progressed further United States Navy Colours were added, principally greens and blues. See Appendix 3.

2. Disruptive Patterns and Standard Schemes

1 Western Approaches Scheme.
Colours:
white, light sea blue, light sea green and darker blues – blue/green panels applied in angular patterns on the lower hull; rest of the ship painted all white.

2A Admiralty Light Disruptive Pattern.

2B Admiralty Intermediate Disruptive Pattern.

2C Admiralty Dark Disruptive Pattern.
Colours:
blues, greys and greens applied in multiple combinations in bold irregular patterns. Used from 1942-1944.

3 Home Fleet Destroyer Scheme.
Colours:
dark blues and greys applied aft and light blues and greys in irregular patterns forward. Unique to destroyers.

4 Admiralty Standard Scheme.
Colours:
sea blue, in a panel, applied over an otherwise all light grey hull; superstructure all light grey. Used from 1944-1945.

5 Admiralty Alternative Scheme.
Colours:
light grey applied on upperworks; dark grey applied on hull and decks. Used from 1944-1945.

Appendix 3

United States Navy Official Measures World War II

United States Navy Camouflage Paint Colours

Title	*Specification*
White (5-U)	52P25
Pale grey (5-P)	52P51
Thayer blue (5-B)	52P47
Light grey (5-L)	52P52
Haze grey (5-H)	52P45
Ocean grey (5-O)	52P46
Navy blue (5-N)	52P44
Deck blue (20-B)	52P43
Blue black (5-TM)	52P42
Dull black (13)	
Pale green (5-PG)	52P53
Light green (5-LG)	52P54
Haze green (5-HG)	52P55
Ocean green (5-OG)	52P56
Navy green (5-NG)	52P57
Deck green (20-G)	52P58
Brown (1A/2A/3A/4A)	
Blue black tinting material (5-TM)	
Green tinting material (5-GTM)	

This list dates from May 1943. Compare with Admiralty Standard Camouflage Colours listed in Appendix 2.

Measure 1 Dark Grey System.
Colours:
dark grey applied overall. Used from late 1940 to early 1942.

Measure 2 Graded System.
Colours:
dark grey, ocean grey and light grey.

Measure 3 Light Grey System.
Colours:
light grey applied overall.

Measure 4 Black System (Destroyers).
Colours:
black applied overall. Unique to destroyers.

Measure 5 Painted False Bow Wave.
Colours:
dark blue and white or light grey, applied with Measures 1, 2 or 3.

Measure 6 6″ Cruiser Painted to Simulate 8″ Cruiser.
Colours:
dark grey and light grey. Unique to cruisers.

Measure 7 4-Funnelled Cruiser Painted to Simulate 4-Funnelled Destroyer.
Colours:
dark grey and light grey. Unique to cruisers.

Measure 8 6″ Cruiser Painted to Simulate 2-Funnelled Destroyer.
Colours:
dark grey and light grey. Unique to cruisers.

Measure 9 Black System (Submarines)
Colours:
black applied overall. Unique to submarines.

Measure 10 Grey System (Submarines)
Colours:
ocean grey applied overall. Unique to submarines.

Measure 11 Sea Blue System.
Colours:
sea blue applied overall, including decks. Used exclusively in the Pacific and Mediterranean; was effective in providing concealment from the air.

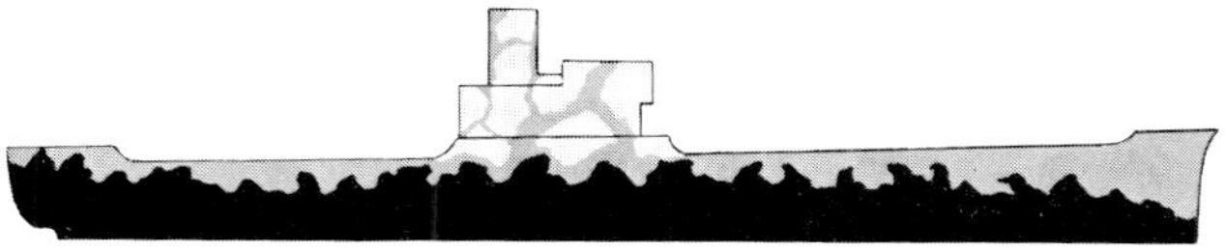

Measure 12 Graded System with Splotches.
Colours:
sea blue and haze grey applied in a mottled pattern on upperworks over solid navy blue or ocean grey on lower hull, areas separated by an irregular line along the weather decks. Used in the Atlantic and Pacific from 1941 to 1943.

Measure 13 Haze Grey System.
Colours:
haze grey applied overall. Considered to be the ideal compromise system for all average conditions.

Measure 14 Ocean Grey System.
Colours:
ocean grey applied overall.

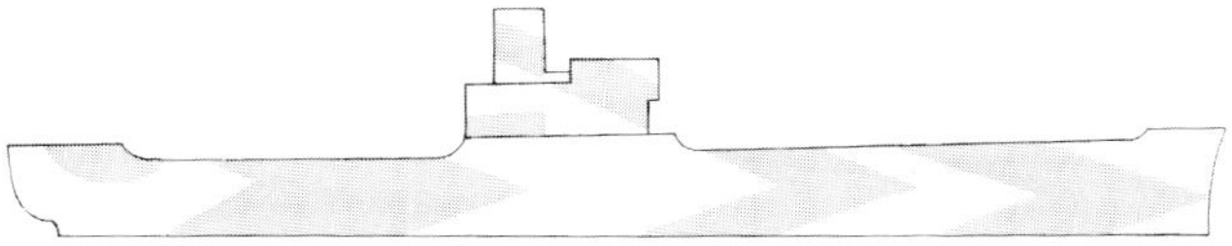

Measure 16 Thayer System.
Colours:
Thayer blue and white applied in chevrons or other patterns of alternating solid colour. Used in the North Atlantic and North Pacific from 1943 to 1944.

Measure 21 Navy Blue System.
Colours:
navy blue applied overall. Used in South and West Pacific from mid-1942 to 1945.

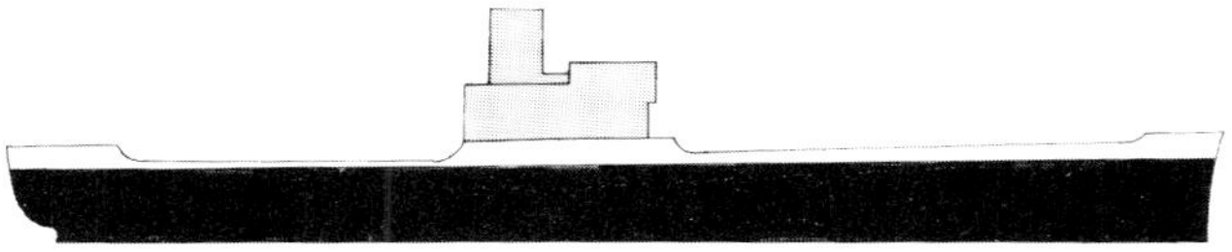

Measure 22 Graded System.
Colours:
haze grey on upper hull and upperworks over navy blue on lower hull, areas separated at the main continuous deck, level with the waterline. Used in the Atlantic and European waters from late 1942 to 1945, in the Pacific from late 1944 to 1945. The most commonly used American camouflage scheme; made it difficult to judge ships' positions relative to the horizon.

Measure 23 Light Grey System.
Colours:
light grey applied overall.

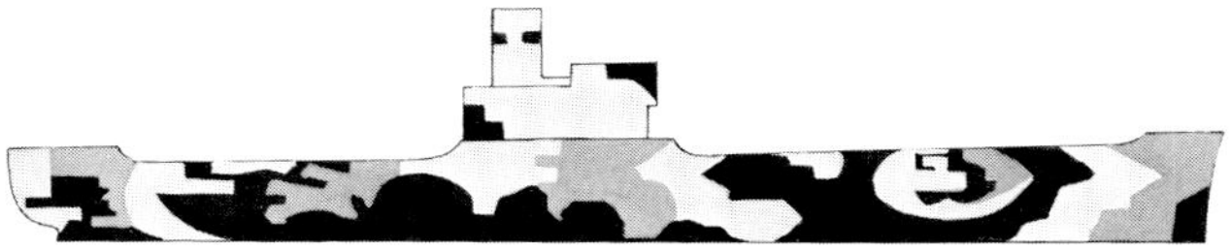

Measure 31 Dark Pattern System.
Colours:
navy green, ocean green, haze green, navy blue, black and brown applied in an irregular pattern similar to that of the Admiralty Disruptive Patterns.

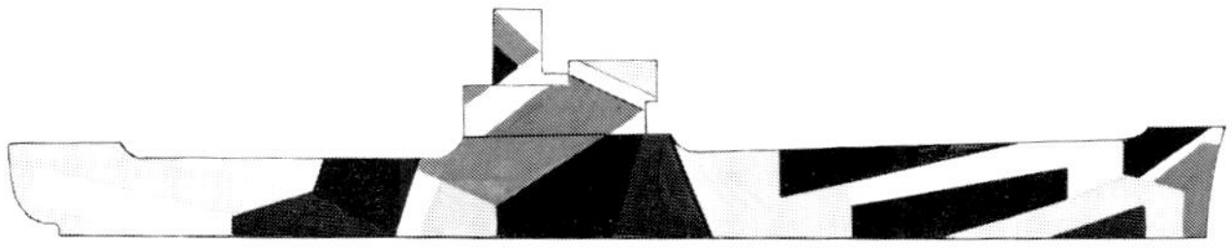

Measure 32 Medium Pattern System.
Colours:
pale grey, haze grey, ocean grey, navy blue and black or sometimes navy green, ocean green and haze green applied in a bold, angular splinter pattern similar to some World War I dazzle designs or in irregular patterns. Used in the Pacific from mid-1944 to 1945.

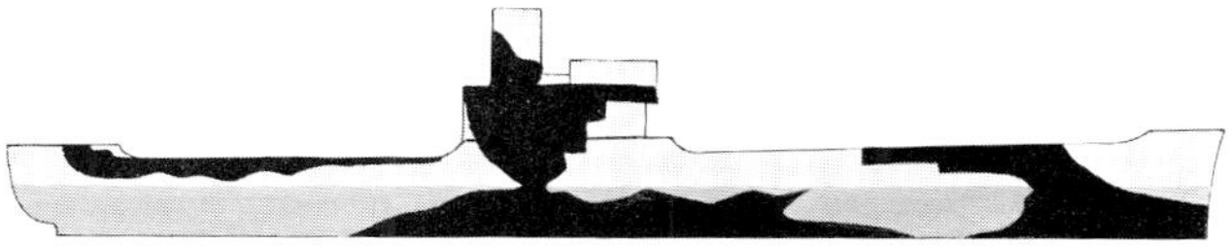

Measure 33 Light Pattern System.
Colours:
pale grey, haze grey and ocean grey or sometimes ocean green and haze green applied in a pattern similar to that of Measure 31, sometimes on only the front half of the ship with an overall light colour from midships aft.

These descriptions are of the official measures; in practice there were numerous variations on the basic themes.

Appendix 4

Comparison of Model Viewing Facilities

Admiralty Dazzle Painting Section
Model Testing Theatre, World War 1

The model testing theatre constructed for the Dazzle Painting Section at the Royal Academy was based on a trestle supported platform. This had a slightly curved surface which inclined downwards to each end, to simulate the horizon. In its centre was a circular turntable on which models could be rotated using pulleys operated by a handle near the viewing position.

A back cloth, painted in skylight colours, was erected at the far end of the platform. The viewing arrangement, situated at the other end, consisted of a periscope shrouded by side and

Fig 1

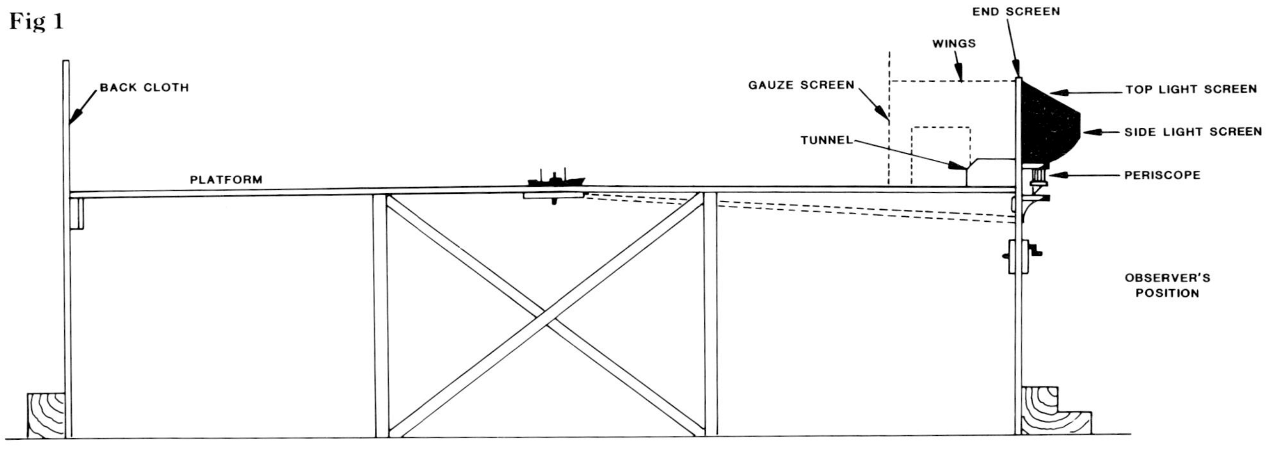

DAZZLE PAINTING SECTION MODEL TESTING THEATRE

top screens painted matt black to shade the observer from obtrusive flair. The periscope was positioned to look along the platform, through an aperture in the end screen through a low tunnel, mounted on the platform side, which was also painted matt black inside. On each side of the tunnel were wings made of opaque white material which were intended to shield the platform from stray room light. These wings were made to various lengths and occasionally extended for the full length of the platform. To simulate atmospheric haze, a gauze screen was placed between the wings across the line of vision. These screens were coloured either light blue or mauve to suit different viewing conditions. Illumination of the model testing theatre was by diffused artificial light.

This model viewing facility, while being an extremely valuable tool for the dazzle painting team, was primitive both in its construction and in its means of simulating and controlling atmospheric conditions.

General Electric Research Laboratories
Naval Camouflage Viewing Range, World War II

Compared with the Royal Academy model testing theatre, the Naval Camouflage Viewing Range was considerably more sophisticated. Constructed for the Naval Section of the Civil Defence Camouflage Establishment at Leamington Spa, the range was based on a large, shallow water tank, about 6in deep, with a weir at each end. The tank was kept full by a pump so that the observer could look from end to end over an uninterrupted expanse of water. Fans were used to provide realistic-looking moving waves on the water surface. The tank was placed in a room that was painted flat white and illuminated by 5ft fluorescent tubes in a special indirect system designed to simulate illumination from a uniformly bright sky. A film studio projector was then used to provide direct sunlight.

The models were placed on a table beyond the tank, supported by blocks at the appropriate height. By moving the models nearer to or further from the observer and by adopting different viewing positions, ranges up to 40 miles could be accurately simulated.

Viewing was by binoculars through a complex arrangement of haze filters and sky screens to synthesise accurately attenuation and veiling in the atmosphere. A night viewing cabin could be added to the standard viewing configuration. Enclosing the observer in darkness, this permitted viewing along the range through an aperture in which neutral density filters were placed to reduce the general illumination to night-time levels.

Fig 2

GENERAL ELECTRIC COMPANY NAVAL CAMOUFLAGE VIEWING RANGE

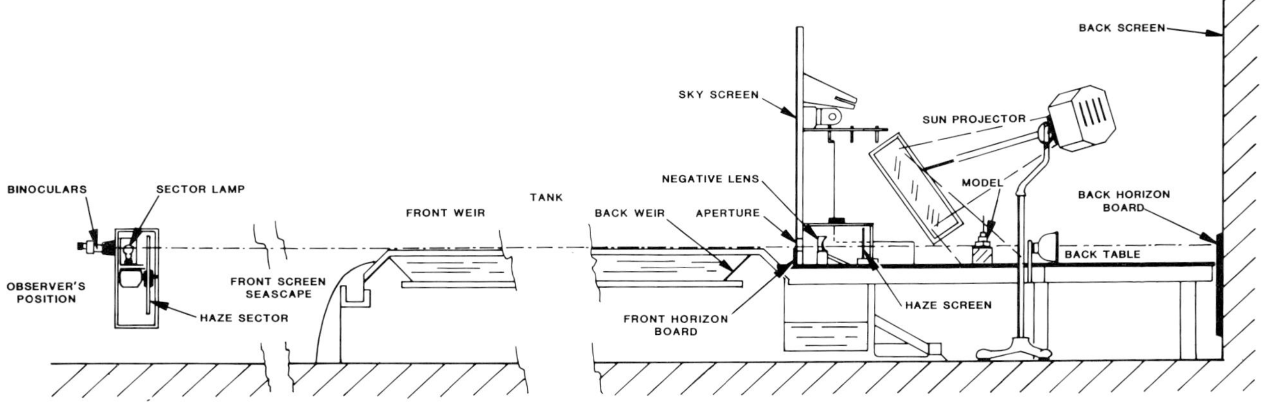

Appendix 5

Biographies of Some Key Camouflage Personalities

Brush, George DeForest (1855-1941)
Born Shelbyville, Tennesee, 20 September 1855.
Figure painter renowned for his fine pictures of American Indian themes. Studied art in Paris. Famous for his studies of protective coloration in the natural world which were applied in various camouflage schemes proposed to the United States Navy from 1899 onwards. Official American camouflage artist during World War I.

Jones, Loyd Ancile (1884-1954)
Born York, Nebraska, 12 April 1884.
Physicist and electrical engineer. Attended Universities of Nebraska and Rochester. Joined Eastman Kodak at Rochester, New York in December 1912. Appointed Director of the Camouflage Research Center in the Eastman Kodak Research Laboratories, serving as a Lieutenant USNR from March 1918 to February 1919. Became Superintendant in Charge of the Physics Department, Eastman Kodak from 1929. Noted for his research into sensitometry (film speed behaviour). This led to the establishment of film speed criterion which has been employed internationally – since 1934 by Eastman Kodak, from 1943 by the American Standards Association and from 1947 by the British Standards Institute.

King, Cecil George Charles (1881-1942)
Born London, 6 August 1881.
Marine artist. Studied art at the Westminster Art School and in Paris. Attached to the Dazzle Painting Section from March 1917 as Lieutenant RNVR. Norman Wilkinson's assistant at the Royal Academy. A regular contributor to the *Illustrated London News* and author of the book, *The History of British Flags*. His work is exhibited at the Imperial War Museum.

Mackay, William Andrew (1878-1939)
Born Philadelphia, Pennsylvania, 10 July 1878.
Painter, muralist and decorative illustrator based in New York. Studied art in Paris and New York. Official American camouflage artist during World War I. Director of the United States Navy Camouflage Training School after World War I.

Schull, Alphonse E (1911-1943)
Born 10 October 1911.
Physicist. Educated at Rutherford College and Armstrong College, Newcastle. Employed by the General Electric Company from April 1937. Designed the haze attenuation and optical systems for the Naval Camouflage Viewing Range at Leamington Spa. Attached to the Admiralty's Directorate of Scientific Research in October 1941. Seconded to the Training and Staff Duties Division, engaged on camouflage research with Lieutenant Oliver Grahame Hall RNVR. Killed during camouflage observation trials off Freetown, Sierra Leone, when the submarine he was aboard, P615, was sunk by a U-boat.

Scott, Peter Markham (1909-)
Born London, 14 September 1909.
Painter, ornithologist and naturalist. Son of Captain Robert Scott, the Antarctic explorer, and Kathleen Bruce, the sculptress. Served with the Royal Naval Volunteer Reserve during World War II. Honorary Director of the Wildfowl Trust, founded by him in 1946. Former Vice President and now Honorary Chairman of the World Wildlife Fund. Has written and illustrated numerous books.

Thayer, Abbott Henderson (1849-1921)
Born Boston, Massachusetts, 12 August 1849.
Leading Idealist painter, celebrated for his figure studies. Pupil at the School of Fine Arts, Paris. Settled in Monadnock, New Hampshire at the beginning of the twentieth century. His concern with colour led him to study and publish on the principles of protective coloration in nature and these were adapted to camouflage techniques in World War I. Advanced camouflage ideas to the United States Navy in 1889 and 1910/1911.

Wadsworth, Edward (1889-1949)
Born Cleckheaton, Yorkshire, 29 October 1889.
Painter and engraver in wood, prominent member of the Vorticist movement. Attended Munich University and the Slade Art School. Attached to the Dazzle Painting Section from March 1917 as Lieutenant RNVR. Executed some of the decorations for the liner *Queen Mary* in 1936. His work is exhibited at the Tate Gallery and the Imperial War Museum.

Warner, Everett Langley (1877-19??)
Born Vinton, Iowa, 16 July 1877.
Landscape painter and water colour artist. Studied art at Washington and New York. Official American camouflage artist during World War I. Attached to the Bureau of Ships' Camouflage Section from 1942 as a civilian consultant.

Wilkinson, Norman (1878-1971)
Born Cambridge, 24 November 1878.
Marine artist, accredited as the inventor of the system of protective naval colouring in World War I, widely known as dazzle painting. Head of the Dazzle Painting Section at the Royal Academy, commissioned as Lieutenant Commander RNVR. Adviser on airfield camouflage to the Air Ministry during World War II. His war paintings from both wars were dedicated to the nation; many are exhibited at the Imperial War Museum and the National Maritime Museum.

Research

1. Bibliography

Braynard, Frank, *Lives of the Liners* (Cornell Maritime Press, 1947)

Cork, Richard, *Vorticism and Abstract Art in the First Machine Age* (Gordon Frazer Gallery, 1976)

Gombrich, E H, *Art and Illusion – A Study in the Psychology of Pictorial Presentation* (Phaidon Press, 1960)

Hartcup, Guy, *Camouflage – A History of Concealment and Deception in War* (David & Charles, 1979)

Jones, Loyd A, *Protective Coloration as a Means of Defense Against Submarines, The Science of Colour* (Eastman Kodak)

Kerr, Graham, *Professor Graham Kerr's Method of Diminishing the Visibility of Ships at a Distance* (published privately, 24 September 1914)

Kochs, A, *Camouflage of Ships* (Group MarRust/FEP, Germany, WWII)

Phillips, Archibald, *Suggestion for the Camouflage or Dazzle of British Merchant Ships in the Great War* (published privately)

Plumridge, Lt Col J H, *Hospital Ships and Ambulance Trains* (Seeley Service, 1975)

Poolman, Kenneth, *Armed Merchant Cruisers – Their Epic Story* (Leo Cooper with Secker & Warburg, 1985)

Rogers, Col H C B OBE, *Troopships and Their History* (Seeley Service, 1963)

Roskam, Albert, *Dazzle Painting – Kunst Als Camouflage* (Stichting Kunstprojecten en Uitgeverij Van Spijk, 1987)

Scott, Peter M, *The Eye of theWind* (1961)

Stevens, W R BSc, AMIEE, FIES and Waldram, J M BSc, F Inst P, FIES, 'Laboratory Techniques in Solving Wartime Visibility Problems' (paper read at the Convention of The Illuminating Engineering Society, 16 May 1946)

Sumrall, Robert F, *Ship Camouflage (WWI): Deceptive Art* (United States Naval Institute Proceedings, July 1971), *Ship Camouflage (WWII): Deceptive Art* (United States Naval Institute Proceedings, February 1973)

Wilkinson, Norman, 'The Dazzle Painting of Ships' (paper read before the North East Coast Institution of Engineers and Shipbuilders at the Victory Meeting, Newcastle-on-Tyne, 10 July 1919), *A Brush With Life* (Seeley Service, 1969)

Williams, David L and De Kerbrech, Richard P, *Damned by Destiny* (Teredo Books, 1981)

Winchester, Clarence (Editor), *Shipping Wonders of the World*

Official publications:

Admiralty: 'History of Sea-Going Camouflage' (RE/CAM/N/22, 15 May 1946), 'Report of the Committee on Dazzle Painting' (31 July 1918)

Comité International de la Croix-Rouge: 'Extracts from the Geneva and Hague Conventions' (Geneva, August 1985)

US Bureau of Ships Camouflage Section: *Handbook of Ship Camouflage* (Navy Dept C&R-4 ATR A-332, 1937), *A Pictorial Report on Japanese Ship Camouflage* (NID 06304/45 ATR A-95/2508, 15 May 1945)

2. Sources

Bundesarchivs, Koblenz, West Germany
Eastman Kodak Research Laboratory, Rochester, New York
International Red Cross, Geneva and London
Imperial War Museum, London
Lloyds Marine Records Collection, Guildhall Library, London
Ministry of Defence, Naval Historical Branch, London
Public Record Office, Kew, London:
- Admiralty Awards for Inventions records – File ADM 245
- Admiralty Research Laboratory correspondence and papers – File ADM 212
- Ministry of Home Security's Dept of Research and Experiment, Camouflage Committee papers – File HO 217

Royal Academy of Arts, London
United States National Archives, Washington, DC
United States Naval Historical Center, Washington, DC
United States Naval Research Library, Washington, DC

Glossary of Terms

1. Camouflage and Technical Terms

Asdic Anglo-French anti-submarine detection device, forerunner of Sonar, named after the Anti-Submarine Detection Investigation Committee. It comprised a transmitter/receiver which sent out undersea sound impulses and picked up the echo if an impulse struck an object. By measuring the time lapse between transmission and reception of the echo, the range of the target could be calculated.

Azimuth Arc of the sky extending from the zenith, the point of the sky directly overhead, to the horizon.

Collimating lens/es Optical system used to produce a parallel or near-parallel beam of light.

Colorimeter Instrument for measuring the intensity of colour.

Colour synthesis The process by which the complete range of visible colours is derived by mixing the three primary wavelengths of light in varying combinations. This is known as additive colour synthesis.
The reproduction of colour in printing and photographic processes is by subtractive colour synthesis in which inks

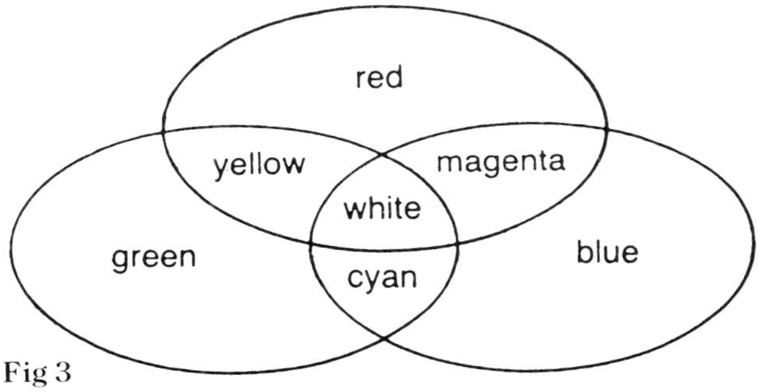

Fig 3

additive colour mixing

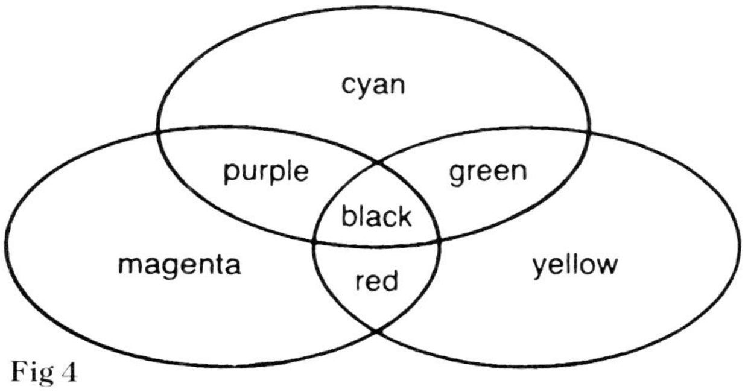

Fig 4

subtractive colour mixing

or dyes of the complementary colours, cyan, magenta and yellow are mixed in varying combinations (Figures 3 and 4).

Colour temperature A standardised value for the colour balance of light sources derived by relating the colour of the light radiating from a heated black box radiator, such as a carbon filament, to its temperature, expressed in degrees Kelvin. The lower the colour temperature the warmer, or redder, the light source: the higher the colour temperature the cooler, or bluer, the light source.

Cones Light sensitive photo-receptor cells in the retina, shaped like cones. Cones are good at recognising colour, but poor at distinguishing changes in brightness (see Rods).

Diffusion The scattering or dispersal of light by material with surface irregularities which cause the refraction of the light rays to occur in many directions or in which suspended particles interfere with the direction of the light rays.

Gestalt psychologists A school of psychologists, notably of the interwar period, who postulated that human beings perceive phenomena, particularly visual phenomena, as relating to an organised configuration, order or shape (German *gestalt*).

Hedgehog Anti-submarine depth charge weapon firing simultaneously, ahead of the attacking ship, a pattern of twenty-four projectiles designed to explode on contact.

Huff Duff Popular name for High Frequency Direction Finder used to locate hostile submarines by taking cross-bearings of a U-boat's radio signals to pinpoint its position. Huff Duff permitted a submarine to be attacked without it getting forewarning that it had been detected.

Incident light The combined light from all sources falling directly upon a surface.

Infra-red radiation Region of invisible, heat generating electromagnetic radiation extending from the red end of the visible spectrum into microwave radio energy.

Light flux Measurement of light energy, expressed in lumens, a unit defined as the amount of light emitted from a standard candle light source into an area of standard square measurement the sides of which are equal in length to the distance of the light source from the centre of the square.

Photometer Instrument for measuring the intensity of light.

Pointillism Method of oil painting with numerous small dots of two or more pure colours which, at a distance, produce the effect of mixed colour. Technique pioneered by the French Impressionist painter Georges Seurat.

Purkinje Effect Effect of the behaviour of the human eye, the ratio of photopic vision to scotopic vision, named after the Czech physiologist Jan Evangelista Purkinje.

Reflection The mirrored deflection of the path of light rays at the point of encountering a surface separating two different media, such as air and metal.

Refraction The deflection of the path of light rays at the point of passage from one transparent medium to another of different density, such as air and water or air and glass.

Rods Light sensitive photo-receptor cells in the retina, shaped like rods. Rods are good at distinguishing changes in brightness but poor at recognising colour (see Cones).

Spectroscope Optical instrument for producing and analysing a spectrum of the light emitted from a source. A calibrated spectroscope is known as a spectrometer.

Squid Anti-submarine depth charge weapon firing simultaneously, ahead of the attacking ship, three

projectiles designed to explode around the U-boat and crack its hull by concussion.
Stereoscopy Vision of an object, by two images, apparently as a solid or in three dimensions.
Visible Spectrum Region of the electromagnetic spectrum of radio energy in which the energy is perceived as visible light. The visible spectrum is bounded at the red end by infra-red radiation and at the violet/blue end by ultra-violet radiation.

2. Terms Used in Naval Camouflage Prepared by the General Electric Company, World War II

(Reproduced by permission of the Public Record Office)

Apparent pattern The pattern seen by an observer, a combination of the painted pattern and the structure pattern.
Apparent tone The reflection factor of a plane lamina parallel to the ship's axis, which appears as the same brightness as the solid ship.
Cast shadow Shadow with well-defined edges formed by direct light from sun or moon.
Conspicuity The degree to which an object attracts the attention of an observer.
Counter-shading A painted pattern in which light tones are used in and around shadows and vice versa so as to make the structure pattern inconspicuous at a distance.
Disappearance range Distance from observer at which observed ship becomes invisible.
Disruptive design A painted pattern, parts of which will match their background, designed to combine with the structure pattern so as to make the identification of class and/or inclination difficult.
Downlight sky brightness ratio Ratio of illumination on two sides of vertical plate facing sun or brightest part of sky.
Effective downlight sky brightness ratio Ratio of illumination on two sides of vertical plate parallel to ship's axis.
Effective horizon sky brightness ratio Ratio of brightness of vertical perfect diffuse reflector parallel to ship's axis, to that of horizon sky beyond ship.
Haze The optical effects of mist.
Highlight Region in which the illumination is increased because the surface is turned towards the light.
Horizon Brightness Factor Ratio of horizon brightness, in stated azimuth, to mean brightness in downlight quadrant of sky.
Horizon position The height above the waterline of a line joining the observer with the horizon; designated positive if the horizon is beyond the ship (ship seen partly againt the sea) and negative if in front of the ship (ship partly hull down).
Horizon sky brightness ratio Ratio of brightness of vertical perfect diffuse reflector facing sun, etc, to that of horizon sky downlight.
Lamina An idealised ship used for calculation of tones; the ship is considered to be a plane lamina parallel to the axis of the real ship.
Mean tone The average reflection factor of a ship or part of a ship having a painted pattern, as calculated from an elevation and without the effects of shadows and highlights.
Mist Optical scattering material present in the atmosphere.
Painted disguise A painted pattern designed so that the apparent pattern of the ship resembles the structure pattern of another ship so as to mislead an observer as to class or inclination.
Painted pattern A pattern of light and dark tones painted on a ship.
Reflection factor The ratio of the total light flux leaving a surface reflection, to that incident upon the surface.
Reflectivity The ratio of the brightness of a surface in a specified direction, to that of a perfect diffuse reflector receiving the same lighting.
Shadow A region in which illumination is produced by obstruction of light by parts of the ship.
Shape shadow lowlight Region in which illumination is reduced because surface is turned away from light.
Sky-sea brightness ratio Ratio of brightnesses of sky and sea at the horizon.
Structure effect The effect of three-dimensional structure of a ship on her appearance in causing shadows, highlights and structure pattern.
Structure factor The factor by which the structure effect changes the apparent tone.
Structure pattern A pattern of shadows and highlights brought about by the effects of three-dimensional structure, not by painting.
Target range Distance of observed ship from observer measured horizontally.
Tone The reflectivity of a painted surface.
Visibility range Disappearance range of large black object seen against horizon sky.